West Nile Virus

Titles in the Diseases & Disorders series include:

Acne
ADHD
Alcoholism
Allergies
Alzheimer's Disease
Amnesia
Anorexia and Bulimia
Anxiety Disorders
Asperger's Syndrome
Asthma
Autism
Autoimmune Disorders
Blindness
Brain Trauma
Brain Tumors
Breast Cancer
Cancer
Cerebral Palsy
Cervical Cancer
Childhood Obesity
Cystic Fibrosis
Dementia
Depression
Diabetes
Epilepsy
Exercise Addiction
Fibromyalgia
Growth Disorders

Hepatitis
Human Papillomavirus (HPV)
Infectious Mononucleosis
Leukemia
Lyme Disease
Malnutrition
Mental Retardation
Migraines
MRSA
Multiple Sclerosis
Osteoporosis
Personality Disorders
Phobias
Plague
Post Traumatic Stress
    Disorder
Prostate Cancer
Radiation Sickness
Sexually Transmitted
    Diseases
Skin Cancer
Speech Disorders
Sports Injuries
Sudden Infant Death
    Syndrome
Thyroid Disorders
Tourette Syndrome
West Nile Virus

DISEASES & DISORDERS

West Nile Virus

Melissa Abramovitz

LUCENT BOOKS
A part of Gale, Cengage Learning

GALE
CENGAGE Learning·

Detroit • New York • San Francisco • New Haven, Conn • Waterville, Maine • London

LIBRARY OF CONGRESS CATALOGING-IN-PUBLICATION DATA

Abramovitz, Melissa, 1954-
  West Nile virus / by Melissa Abramovitz.
     p. cm. -- (Diseases & disorders)
  Includes bibliographical references and index.
  ISBN 978-1-4205-0936-6 (hardcover)
  1. West Nile fever--Juvenile literature. 2. West Nile virus--Juvenile literature. I. Title.
  RA644.W47A25 2013
  614.5'8856--dc23

                                                          2012034405

Lucent Books
27500 Drake Rd.
Farmington Hills, MI 48331

ISBN-13: 978-1-4205-0936-6
ISBN-10: 1-4205-0936-5

Printed in the United States of America
1 2 3 4 5 6 7 16 15 14 13 12

Table of Contents

"The Most Difficult Puzzles Ever Devised"

Charles Best, one of the pioneers in the search for a cure for diabetes, once explained what it is about medical research that intrigued him so. "It's not just the gratification of knowing one is helping people," he confided, "although that probably is a more heroic and selfless motivation. Those feelings may enter in, but truly, what I find best is the feeling of going toe to toe with nature, of trying to solve the most difficult puzzles ever devised. The answers are there somewhere, those keys that will solve the puzzle and make the patient well. But how will those keys be found?"

Since the dawn of civilization, nothing has so puzzled people— and often frightened them, as well—as the onset of illness in a body or mind that had seemed healthy before. A seizure, the inability of a heart to pump, the sudden deterioration of muscle tone in a small child—being unable to reverse such conditions or even to understand why they occur was unspeakably frustrating to healers. Even before there were names for such conditions, even before they were understood at all, each was a reminder of how complex the human body was, and how vulnerable.

While our grappling with understanding diseases has been frustrating at times, it has also provided some of humankind's most heroic accomplishments. Alexander Fleming's accidental discovery in 1928 of a mold that could be turned into penicillin has resulted in the saving of untold millions of lives. The isolation of the enzyme insulin has reversed what was once a death sentence for anyone with diabetes. There have been great strides in combating conditions for which there is not yet a cure, too. Medicines can help AIDS patients live longer, diagnostic tools such as mammography and ultrasounds can help doctors find tumors while they are treatable, and laser surgery techniques have made the most intricate, minute operations routine.

This "toe-to-toe" competition with diseases and disorders is even more remarkable when seen in a historical continuum. An astonishing amount of progress has been made in a very short time. Just two hundred years ago, the existence of germs as a cause of some diseases was unknown. In fact, it was less than 150 years ago that a British surgeon named Joseph Lister had difficulty persuading his fellow doctors that washing their hands before delivering a baby might increase the chances of a healthy delivery (especially if they had just attended to a diseased patient)!

Each book in Lucent's Diseases and Disorders series explores a disease or disorder and the knowledge that has been accumulated (or discarded) by doctors through the years. Each book also examines the tools used for pinpointing a diagnosis, as well as the various means that are used to treat or cure a disease. Finally, new ideas are presented—techniques or medicines that may be on the horizon.

Frustration and disappointment are still part of medicine, for not every disease or condition can be cured or prevented. But the limitations of knowledge are being pushed outward constantly; the "most difficult puzzles ever devised" are finding challengers every day.

A Spreading Invasion

In August 1999 eight people in New York City developed an unusual type of encephalitis (brain inflammation). The patients ranged in age from fifty-eight to eighty-seven. All were previously fairly healthy, and all had fever followed by changes in mental function, which is typical in encephalitis. But seven of the eight also had severe muscle weakness, which is unusual in encephalitis, and three had Guillain-Barré-like symptoms, which are also atypical. Guillain-Barré syndrome is characterized by sudden weakness or paralysis in the arms, legs, face, and muscles that control breathing. Four patients went on to develop paralysis so severe that they could not breathe on their own and had to be placed on mechanical ventilators.

Investigating the Mystery

The patients' doctors alerted the New York City Department of Health, and epidemiologists (doctors who specialize in tracking down the causes and spread of mysterious or infectious diseases) began trying to determine what was causing these strange varieties of encephalitis. The first step involved analyzing what the patients had in common. Blood tests and tests on the cerebrospinal fluid, which surrounds the brain and spinal cord, revealed that all the patients had an unidentified viral infection. Investigators also discovered that all the patients lived within a 16-square-mile area (41.4 sq. km) in the Queens section of New York City, and all reported that they had been outdoors on recent evenings. This suggested that mosquitoes, which carry many viruses and are most active in the early evening, may have transmitted whichever virus was causing the illness.

Scientists analyzed standing water near each of the patients' homes and discovered culex mosquito larvae. As more reports of other people with similar symptoms came into the health department, further data revealed that all the patients had recently been near mosquito breeding sites. During the remainder of 1999, a total of sixty-two people in New York City were affected by the mysterious illness, and seven died.

Physicians began testing patients' blood and cerebrospinal fluid for viruses commonly spread by mosquitoes. They found that all had antibodies to Saint Louis encephalitis virus, the most common mosquito-borne virus in the United States. Antibodies are chemicals produced by the immune system to attack specific antigens (foreign proteins or organisms such as viruses). The presence of these antibodies suggested that Saint Louis encephalitis virus was probably the cause of the patients' symptoms.

Further Clues

The mystery, however, had not yet been solved. Around the same time the odd encephalitis-like infections were occurring in humans, public health officials became aware that large numbers of wild birds, especially crows, were dying in the same area. Several resident birds in the Queens and Bronx zoos also died from unknown causes. Epidemiologists did not link the illnesses in birds and humans initially. According to the book *West Nile Virus Outbreak: Lessons for Public Health Preparedness*, "Large numbers of dying birds and an unusual cluster of human cases were at first viewed as separate events. Gradually, as an increasing number of laboratories became involved to conduct further testing on human, animal, and mosquito samples, the linkages became clear."[1]

Tracy McNamara, a pathologist at the Bronx Zoo, was one of the first to suspect a connection between the human outbreak

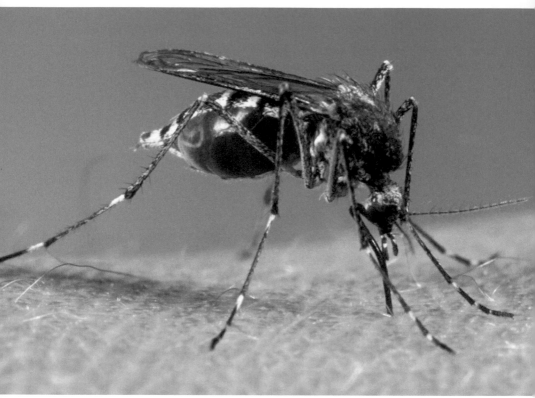

The *Aedes aegypti* mosquito transmits the West Nile virus.

and bird deaths when she discovered during autopsies that the dead birds at her zoo died from encephalitis. As a *Smithsonian* magazine article states, "The coincidence was too much for McNamara to ignore."[2] McNamara explains, "The fact is, I had a bunch of dead birds that had died of encephalitis at the same time that people had encephalitis.'"[3] Knowing that birds do not die from Saint Louis encephalitis virus, McNamara suspected that the human laboratory results identifying this virus were in error. She sent samples of the dead birds' brain tissue to the National Veterinary Services Laboratory in Ames, Iowa, which found that the birds were infected with West Nile virus (WNV). McNamara and other scientists were amazed by this finding because WNV had never before been seen in North America; only in Europe, Asia, Africa, the Middle East, and Australia.

The Centers for Disease Control and Prevention (CDC) retested the human blood samples and found that the real culprit was WNV in these cases as well. The previous results indicating Saint Louis encephalitis virus were in error, most likely because the two viruses look very similar and are closely related.

Part of the Mystery Solved

Biologists began testing more than three hundred thousand mosquitoes in New York and discovered that eight species were infected with WNV. This explained how people and birds were becoming infected from mosquito bites, but health experts were still puzzled about how the virus suddenly appeared in the United States. No one ever solved this part of the mystery, but epidemiologists believe that either imported birds or mosquitoes that got into cargo from other countries were responsible. Indeed, as worldwide travel has increased in recent years, people, animals, and cargo from around the world have spread numerous disease-causing pathogens to America.

Since 1999 WNV has spread rapidly throughout both North and South America. By 2001 cases in twenty-seven U.S. states had been reported, and by 2002 WNV had spread to forty-nine states and Washington, D.C., as well as to Canada and Mexico, affecting thousands of people, birds, and other animals. As of June 2012 the CDC estimated that over thirty thousand people in the United States had been infected, with almost thirteen thousand of these infections being severe and over twelve hundred people dying. WNV continues its invasion across the Western Hemisphere, and public health officials are engaged in an ongoing battle to control this frightening virus.

CHAPTER ONE

What Is West Nile Virus?

As WNV has appeared in many new places throughout the world, scientists have learned a great deal about its characteristics. The term *West Nile virus* refers to both a type of virus and to the disease caused by this virus. Medical experts have focused on increasing their understanding of both the virus itself and its effects on people and animals.

Viruses are submicroscopic organisms that can only be seen with an electron microscope. Scientists measure their size in nanometers; a nanometer is one-billionth of a meter. Viruses range in size from 5 to 300 nanometers. These tiny organisms are composed mostly of deoxyribonucleic acid (DNA) or ribonucleic acid (RNA). DNA molecules make up the building blocks of the genes that determine the nature and function of living cells. DNA copies its genetic instructions onto RNA molecules, which then translate the instructions so cells can read them.

Besides DNA or RNA, viruses also consist of a protein outer shell called a capsid. Some viruses also have a second protein layer called a core inside the capsid, and some have a fat/protein covering known as an envelope outside the capsid. Scientists classify viruses based on their size, shape, presence or absence of an envelope, and type of genome (whether it is made of DNA or RNA and how many strands of DNA or RNA it has). WNV is classified as a flavivirus in the virus family Flaviviridae.

The Latin word *flavus* means "yellow," and this group of viruses is named for the yellow fever virus that is one of its best-known members. Flaviviruses are made of a single strand of RNA and have an outer envelope. They range in size from 40 to 60 nanometers and are classified as small viruses.

As tiny as viruses are, they cause widespread disease and suffering. They can infect many types of plants and animals with a range of illnesses, some of which are fatal. Infecting living cells is the means by which viruses live and reproduce. They cannot live on their own, and once they infect, or get inside a cell, they replicate to make more viruses. Viruses accomplish this by taking over the cell's machinery and using it to manufacture new virus components. Then the virus assembles these components into new viruses, which leave the cell and enter other cells.

Characteristics of West Nile Virus

Although all viruses can infect living cells, different types of viruses have various characteristics that distinguish them from one another. To begin with, different viruses are adept at infecting different types of cells. For example, WNV infects nerve cells (neurons) and can thus cause diseases associated with the nervous system. Whichever cells it infects, once a virus is inside the body, the host's immune system produces antibodies and other immune chemicals, along with immune cells, to kill the invader. Eventually, either the immune system frees the body of the virus by destroying it or the virus overpowers the immune system and continues to replicate. This can result in the host's death.

Besides infecting different types of cells, different viruses enter living creatures by different means. Some, for example, enter through the nose or mouth. Others, like WNV, enter the bloodstream through a mosquito bite. WNV and similar viruses are thus known as arboviruses because they are transmitted by bloodsucking arthropods such as mosquitoes, ticks, or fleas.

WNV was so named because doctors led by Kenneth Smithburn of the Rockefeller Foundation first discovered it in 1937 in the West Nile region of Uganda. While studying yellow fever

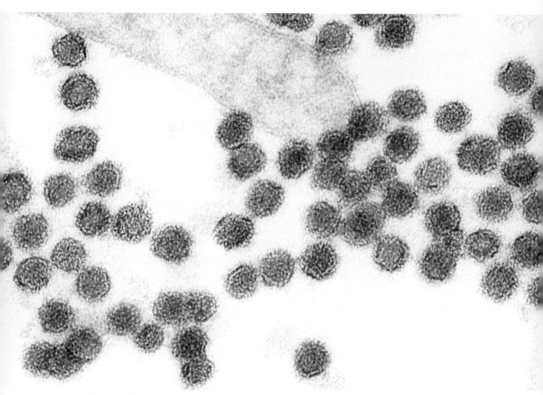

A colored electron micrograph of the West Nile virus, a type of flavivirus that infects nerves cells and causes inflammation.

and related diseases, Smithburn took blood samples from a thirty-seven-year-old woman with a high fever. Her blood contained a virus the doctors had never seen before, and they named it after the area where the woman lived.

Smithburn and his colleagues injected the woman's blood into laboratory animals and found that it caused weakness, paralysis, encephalitis, coma, and death in most of the animals. Examinations of the creatures' brains after death showed swelling, lesions (sores), and nerve cell damage. The virus appeared not to affect organs other than the brain.

Later studies found that WNV was very similar to other flaviviruses such as Saint Louis encephalitis virus, Japanese encephalitis virus, and Murray Valley encephalitis virus. These viruses look similar under an electron microscope and can cause similar symptoms, so distinguishing them from each other can be challenging, as evidenced in 1999 when investigators initially believed Saint Louis encephalitis virus was responsible for the New York WNV epidemic.

Ongoing Outbreaks

Since WNV was first identified, health experts have investigated many outbreaks of WNV disease, particularly in areas where the virus is endemic (always present). These areas were primarily in the Middle East and Africa prior to 1999. Many people in endemic areas have antibodies to WNV in their blood, even when they show no symptoms of illness. For instance, studies in the 1950s showed that about 60 percent of the people living near the Nile River in Egypt had such antibodies, indicating that they had been previously infected. Many had been infected during childhood and had only a mild form of the disease or were unaware that they had been infected at all. Once an individual becomes infected, antibodies can remain in the blood for a long time and give the person immunity from later infection.

West Nile Virus: Approximate Geographic Range, 2003

Taken from: Centers for Disease Control and Prevention. www.cdc.gov.

Prior to the late 1990s most WNV outbreaks occurred in rural areas, and most infected people developed only minor aches and pains and low-grade fever. According to an article in the *Cleveland Clinic Journal of Medicine,* "West Nile fever was initially considered a universally mild, self-limited disease, marked by several days of fever and other 'flu-like' symptoms. . . . In the 1950s West Nile virus showed that it could cause neurologic disease, although rarely."[4] But beginning around 1996, health experts in Romania, Russia, Israel, and several other places reported that outbreaks were centered in urban areas where they had never before been seen. Many people affected in these newer outbreaks showed severe neurological (nervous system) symptoms such as those later seen in the New York City outbreak. The subsequent spread of WNV throughout the United States followed this pattern of increasingly severe disease. In 2006, for example, of 4,261 reported WNV infections in the United States, 1,455 involved serious illness.

Cases in animals, too, have become increasingly severe or fatal, and more and more types of animals are being infected. Prior to outbreaks in Israel, Romania, and Russia in the late 1990s, large numbers of birds did not become seriously ill or die from WNV. But in these outbreaks, and later in outbreaks in the United States, thousands of birds died. Horses, too, have been seriously impacted by WNV in recent years; in fact, about 40 percent of infected horses die from the virus or must be euthanized because of severe disability. Many other wild and domestic animals have also suffered severe disability or died. Dogs, cats, skunks, squirrels, and bats are among those affected in recent years. Prior to 2002, infections in reptiles had never been reported, but in 2002 numerous alligators at alligator farms in Florida became infected and died. Veterinarians determined that mosquitoes can bite alligators around the eyes or on the soft underbelly and inject the virus.

More Dangerous Virus Strains
Scientists attribute the increasingly serious cases of WNV illness to virus mutations (genetic changes) that have made the virus more virulent, or potent. Mutations produce new strains,

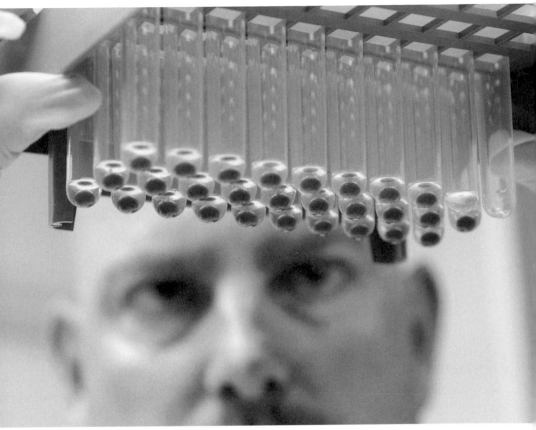

A lab technician screens blood for West Nile virus. Several tests are available to screen for the virus.

or varieties, of the virus that then spread and displace previously active strains. For instance, the WNV strain known as NY99 found in people and animals in New York in 1999 was identical to one found in earlier epidemics in Israel and Europe. By 2002 this strain had mutated into a new strain called WN02, which was transmitted more efficiently by local mosquitoes in the United States and which was even more likely to cause serious illness. By 2005 most new cases of WNV in the United States were caused by the WN02 strain. The ability of RNA viruses like WNV to mutate quickly is one factor that makes them so difficult to combat. According to researchers at the University of New Mexico School of Medicine, "RNA viruses possess an extraordinary capacity to adapt to changing environments due to their high mutation rate."[5] This poses a challenge to both epidemiologists and doctors as they track strains of WNV and attempt to treat patients.

There have been changes in the major types, or lineages, of WNV, as well as in the strains of the virus. Virologists divide viruses into lineages, as well as into strains that fit into the main lineage categories but that have minor genetic variations. There are two major WNV lineages—lineage 1 and lineage 2— that cause human disease, though a total of six different lineages have been identified. Scientists identify lineages and strains using gene sequencing and mapping techniques such as polymerase chain reaction that reveal DNA and RNA sequences that characterize different organisms. Among the laboratory tests used to identify WNV are the Procleix West Nile Virus Assay, the Procleix TIGRIS System, and the Cobas TAQ Screen WNV Test.

Prior to 2004, scientists believed that only lineage 1 WNVs caused human disease. Researchers identified various strains of lineage 1 WNV in Africa, Asia, Europe, the Middle East, the United States, and Australia. Lineage 2 viruses had been seen in animals in Africa but did not seem to infect humans or to cause serious illness. But since 2004, cases of severe disease in humans and animals have been attributed to lineage 2 strains, and scientists now know that both lineage 1 and lineage 2 viruses are capable of mutating rapidly when they appear in new places. In 2010, for example, a major WNV outbreak in Greece was caused by lineage 2 viruses, and in 2011 the first lineage 2 case of human illness in Italy was documented. Other cases have been seen in Hungary, Romania, Russia, and South Africa. A January 2012 article in the journal *Veterinary Research* states, "At least two lineage 2 strains are circulating in Europe causing severe disease in humans."[6]

Degrees and Types of Illness

Even very virulent lineages or strains of WNV, however, do not sicken everyone who becomes infected. In fact, about 80 percent of the people infected with any strain of WNV show no

A Risk Factor for Severe West Nile Virus Illness

Studies on mice and humans by Philip M. Murphy and his colleagues at the NIAID in 2005 showed that those lacking a cell surface protein called CCR5 were very likely to become ill or die from a WNV infection. CCR5 allows several types of immune cells to enter the central nervous system and then kill the virus. A lack of CCR5 results from defects in a gene that instructs cells to produce the protein. The CCR5 defects were the first known genetic susceptibility factors for WNV illness.

Other research has shown that CCR5 has the opposite effect on people's resistance to HIV, the virus that causes AIDS. Those who lack CCR5 are less likely to develop AIDS when exposed to HIV. This knowledge led to the use of a CCR5-blocking drug called maraviroc in some AIDS patients. The use of maraviroc, however, has led to some concern among doctors about the possibility of increasing patients' susceptibility to severe WNV illness. Some doctors have suggested that people taking this drug take extra care to avoid being bitten by mosquitoes. Others, such as a group of NIAID researchers, suggested in a January 2012 article in the *Journal of Infectious Diseases* "that if a patient who is currently taking Maraviroc does test positive for WNV infection or displays characteristic symptoms during an outbreak that the drug be held until the infection is cleared."

Jean K. Lim et al. "CCR5 Deficiency Is a Risk Factor for Early Clinical Manifestations of West Nile Virus Infection, but Not for Infection Per Se." *Journal of Infectious Diseases*, January 15, 2012. www.ncbi.nlm.nih.gov/pmc/articles/PMC2934858.

symptoms. Among those who do get sick, generally about 5 percent have severe illness. After the 1999 outbreak in New York ended, the city health department and the CDC performed blood tests on a random sample of people living in Queens to determine whether more people in addition to those who showed symptoms had been infected. According to the

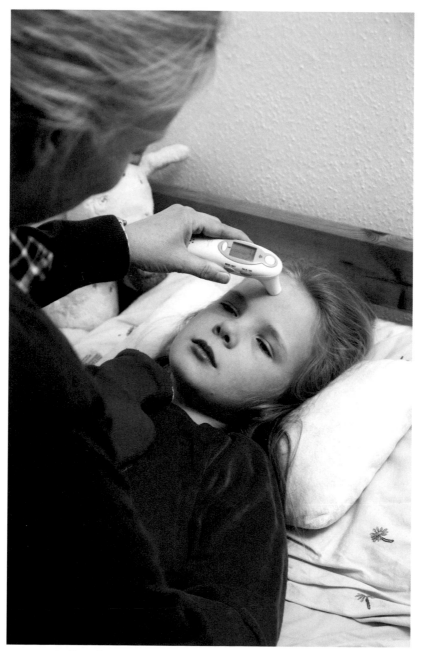

West Nile fever's symptoms include headache, fever, body aches, and sometimes a rash, nausea, vomiting, eye pain, or swollen lymph nodes. Unfortunately these symptoms are shared by many other diseases, complicating the diagnosis.

book *West Nile Virus Outbreak,* "The results of this serosurvey (in which a blood test for West Nile antibodies is performed) revealed that between 1.2 and 4.1 percent of the population in the area surveyed had been infected with West Nile virus."[7] This indicated that many, many infected people never even knew they had contracted the virus because they did not feel ill.

Among those who do become ill from WNV, symptoms appear after an incubation period—the time after infection when the virus begins to take over the body's cells but the victim does not appear ill—which is from 3 to 15 days after contracting the virus. Once symptoms begin to appear, they can range from mild to severe to life-threatening. The National Institutes of Health states, "Scientists do not know why some people infected with West Nile virus have no symptoms or a mild flu-like illness, while in others the virus invades the central nervous system and causes paralysis or coma."[8]

Doctors divide people who develop symptoms into two groups. They refer to those in the first group as having West Nile fever, which involves mild flu-like symptoms, including headache, fever, body aches, and sometimes a rash, nausea, vomiting, eye pain, or swollen lymph nodes. These symptoms usually go away within a few days.

The second category of patients is classified as suffering from neuroinvasive WNV disease, since the virus invades the central nervous system (the brain and spinal cord). The virus accomplishes this by crossing the blood-brain barrier, which is a biological mechanism in the body that prevents most organisms and poisons in the blood from entering the nervous system in order to protect this vital command center. Tightly packed cells that line the capillaries (small blood vessels) in the central nervous system regulate the blood-brain barrier by being selectively permeable; that is, these cells allow substances, such as nutrients, to pass through but prevent potentially damaging substances or pathogens from crossing between the blood system and the nervous system. However, sometimes small viruses such as WNV slip by and infect the central nervous system. The severity of illness they cause depends partly on how many virus particles get in and partly on where they settle.

Types of Neuroinvasive WNV

There are four main types of neuroinvasive WNV. All can be fatal. These illnesses can last for weeks or months and can also result in permanent disability. The first type, West Nile encephalitis, is the most severe form of WNV disease and affects 60 to 75 percent of people with neuroinvasive WNV. It involves inflammation, or swelling, of the brain. Symptoms depend on which part of the brain is affected. If, for example, the cerebral cortex, which governs thinking and reasoning, is affected, the patient may become confused or disoriented or have memory loss, in addition to having other WNV symptoms of fever, aches, and so on. If the cerebellum, which regulates movement, is impacted, the person may not be able to walk or move various muscles. Inflammation in other areas of the brain can lead to seizures, weakness, coma, or inflamed eyes.

Some people with West Nile encephalitis develop symptoms similar to those seen in Guillain-Barré syndrome, which occurs when antibodies and white blood cells damage cells that protect neurons. This results in disruptions in nerve signal transmission that can lead to sudden paralysis in the face, limbs, or breathing muscles.

The second type of neuroinvasive WNV is West Nile meningitis, or inflammation of the meninges (the lining of the brain). This type affects 25 to 35 percent of patients with neuroinvasive disease. Symptoms may include a stiff neck, sensitivity to light, and seizures, along with other typical WNV symptoms. When both the brain and the meninges are inflamed, the condition is called meningoencephalitis; this is the third type of neuroinvasive WNV.

The fourth type is West Nile poliomyelitis. This is an inflammation of the spinal cord that produces symptoms similar to those seen in polio, such as sudden weakness, paralysis, and pain. As with other forms of neuroinvasive disease, if the breathing muscles are paralyzed, respiratory failure can result.

Scientists at the Pasteur Institute in Paris, France, found that a defect in a gene they named the West Nile gene was the reason some West Nile–infected mice died while others without the defect did not.

West Nile poliomyelitis did not appear in the United States until 2002; the other types of neuroinvasive WNV affected people in the original 1999 outbreak. As West Nile poliomyelitis began to appear in 2002, more and more patients with the other types of WNV neuroinvasive disease began developing paralysis and showed other unusual neurological symptoms. As Sidney Houff of Loyola University Medical Center in Illinois reported, "We have begun to see patients with optic nerve disease, anterior horn cell disease and paralysis, Parkinson's-like syndrome and so forth during the acute illness."[9] Optic nerve disease affects vision, and anterior horn cell disease and Parkinson's impact movement. Doctors attributed these new symptoms to the new WN02 virus.

Factors Affecting Disease Severity

How sick an individual becomes after being infected with WNV is influenced by several factors in addition to the strain of the virus. These factors include age, genetics, the presence of other illnesses, and nutrition. Although anyone of any age can become severely ill, people over age fifty are at highest risk for serious illness, lasting disability, or death from WNV. In fact, states the CDC, "age is by far the most important risk factor for developing neuroinvasive WNV infection."[10] Doctors believe this may be because parts of the immune system that fight viruses may weaken as people age.

An individual's nutritional status also affects his or her susceptibility to severe illness. People who are well-nourished are less likely to become seriously ill, probably because nourishment affects overall health. A balanced diet provides the nutrients the body needs to manufacture necessary chemicals and cells, including immune chemicals and cells, so the entire body has the building blocks it needs to function optimally. A strong immune system, in particular, is capable of fighting off an invading virus.

Those who have chronic illnesses such as diabetes or heart disease, on the other hand, are much more likely to experience severe WNV disease or to die from the infection. This is because chronic diseases tend to weaken the immune system, leaving viruses more likely to overwhelm the body's defenses. For instance, Kadi, a WNV patient who previously had polio as a child and who suffered lasting effects called post-polio syndrome, became severely ill from WNV, in large part because polio had weakened her nervous system. She did recover from the WNV infection but was left with lasting weakness in her legs that was exacerbated by her post-polio syndrome.

Genetics also plays a role in determining illness severity, in part because the genes people and animals inherit influence how their immune system responds to infection. Researchers have found that mice that possess some genetic traits show no symptoms when infected with WNV. Some mice without these traits become mildly ill, and mice that have other types of genetic mutations become very sick. Mice with one particular mutation inevitably die within two weeks of infection. Scientists at the Pasteur Institute in Paris, France, determined that a defect in a gene they named the West Nile gene was responsible for the deaths of these mice. The defect blocks a protein that would normally prevent the virus from reproducing. Without the protein, the virus replicates uncontrollably and overwhelms the creatures' immune systems.

In 2008 scientists at Washington University in St. Louis, Missouri, discovered that mice with defects in the toll-like receptor 3 (TLR3) gene, which generates immune chemicals such as interleukin-6, are also susceptible to getting severe WNV illness. Since TLR3 activity is often reduced in elderly people, the researchers have proposed that this may account for the increased incidence of severe WNV disease in people over fifty.

In humans, scientists have found that several genetic characteristics contribute to susceptibility to severe WNV illness. Researchers at the National Institute of Allergy and Infectious Diseases (NIAID) found that a mutation called the delta 32 mutation in the chemokine receptor 5 (CCR5) gene, which governs the action of white blood cells called lymphocytes, quadruples people's risk of severe WNV illness. Other studies indicate that people whose bodies produce fewer than normal T lymphocytes, a type of white blood cell important in fighting viruses, and those who produce low levels of immune chemicals called interferons, are also highly likely to become seriously ill.

Other genetic influences in humans include a mutation in the OAS gene that encodes instructions for production of the immune chemical oligoadenylate synthetase. Investigators at Baylor College of Medicine in Houston found that 84 percent of patients with severe WNV illness had this mutation, whereas only 48 percent of patients with mild disease had it. OAS mutations in horses have also been linked to a tendency to develop serious illness.

Doctors believe that genetic factors also influence the likelihood that WNV will cross the blood-brain barrier and cause neuroinvasive disease. However, they have not yet discovered which genes or mutations are responsible.

Even though knowledge of personal characteristics such as age, genetics, and nutrition can help doctors predict the likelihood of severe WNV disease, these characteristics are not always reliable indicators. Young, healthy people can also become seriously ill or die, and as with older people, this depends partly on the virus strain that infects them. But even pinpointing the virus strain does not tell experts what will happen to a particular patient, as individual responses to the same strain vary widely.

Diagnosing West Nile Virus

Although identifying the virus strain does not reliably allow doctors to predict whether or not an infected person will become severely ill, sometimes these tests are used to confirm a suspected diagnosis of WNV. Most laboratories, however, are not equipped to test for virus strains, and these tests are mainly used to help epidemiologists track a WNV invasion in a given area. In most instances, doctors confirm a suspected WNV diagnosis by testing patients' blood or cerebrospinal fluid for antibodies to the virus or for proteins, or antigens, that sit on the surface of the virus. According to an article in the journal *Clinical Laboratory Medicine*, "To date, the most consistent way to verify WNV infection is serology [blood or cerebrospinal

Diagnosing West Nile Virus with ELISA

West Nile virus antigen-specific ELISA is the most reliable test currently used to confirm a diagnosis of WNV. ELISA is a general type of laboratory test that measures whether a specific antibody associated with a virus or other organism is found in a patient's blood. If the antibody is present, it means the person is infected with the virus.

To perform an ELISA test, laboratory technicians take a blood sample and remove the blood cells, leaving only the liquid portion of the blood, known as plasma. They then introduce the target antigen (virus) into the sample. If antibodies to WNV are present, they will hook onto the antigen, forming what is known as an immune complex. Scientists can detect immune complexes using a laboratory-made antibody attached to an enzyme (a chemical that stimulates a chemical reaction). If immune complexes are present, they will bind to the laboratory-created antibody, and if this happens, the enzyme makes the mixture turn colors. The presence of immune complexes is thus used to assess indirectly whether or not the virus is present in the blood.

A lab technician performs an ELISA test on a blood sample. The test is the most reliable one currently used to diagnose West Nile virus.

fluid tests]. WNV antigen-specific enzyme-linked immunosor-
bent assay (ELISA) confirms infection [most often]."[11]

Other types of tests are used to diagnose different types of
neuroinvasive WNV. Imaging tests such as computed tomogra-
phy (CT) or magnetic resonance imaging (MRI) can reveal inflammation in the brain or meninges. CT scans are X-rays that
give three-dimensional computerized images of internal organs.
MRI machines use magnetic fields and radio waves to give similar pictures. But without tests like ELISA to confirm the presence of WNV, these imaging tests cannot distinguish other types
of encephalitis or meningitis from that caused by WNV.

Since WNV arrived in the United States, public health experts
have made it a priority to encourage doctors to test for WNV
antigens or antibodies. Testing is emphasized in the summer

A technician takes a blood sample from a man to run a screen for
West Nile virus. The most consistent way to verify West Nile infection
is by testing blood or cerebrospinal fluid.

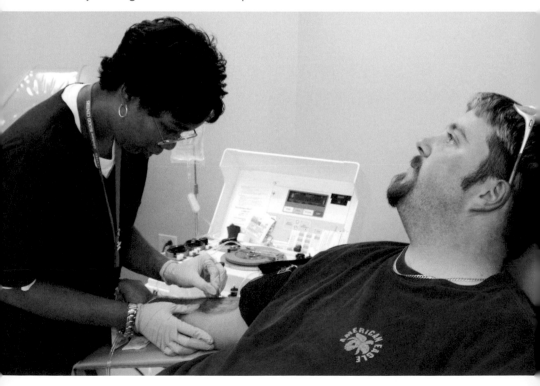

months, but the CDC advises that doctors should always be on the lookout for WNV symptoms and test accordingly. The CDC states: "Because year-round transmission is possible in Southern states, WNV should always be considered in persons with unexplained encephalitis or meningitis."[12] Because WNV is an infectious disease, once a doctor diagnoses it, he or she is required to report the diagnosis to public health departments. This way, these agencies can track the incidence and spread of the disease to help with control efforts.

CHAPTER TWO

How West Nile Virus Is Spread

After the initial 1999 outbreak in New York, WNV spread rapidly throughout the United States and into Canada, Mexico, and Central and South America. Within a year of the outbreak, the number of WNV infections in the United States increased by nearly 2,000 percent. By 2012 over thirty thousand human infections, nearly thirteen thousand of which were severe, and over twelve hundred deaths had been reported in the United States. Thousands of animal infections and deaths have occurred as well, and the spread of the virus shows no sign of stopping. According to an article in the journal *Molecular Ecology*, WNV is now "the world's most widely distributed arbovirus."[13] WNV is also now considered to be endemic in the United States.

The Primary Host

By tracking WNV strains in infected animals and people, scientists have determined how the virus has spread and what factors contribute to the speed of transmission. WNV infections begin in birds, which are known as the primary or amplifying hosts. The first evidence that birds were associated with spreading WNV was discovered by scientists performing studies in Egypt in 1952 and 1954. The researchers found antibodies to WNV in several species of birds, and subsequent studies showed that human epidemics followed bird illnesses and deaths in particular areas. Since the studies in Egypt, biologists have identified over three hundred species of birds that can carry WNV. Sometimes the virus kills the birds; other times it makes them temporarily sick. The birds that survive are mostly responsible for spreading the virus, and in many places the spread of WNV to other animals and people follows bird migration patterns. However, infected birds do not directly transmit the virus to other animals and people. Instead, mosquitoes that bite an infected bird become infected and then spread WNV to other organisms.

Crows have been widely sickened by West Nile virus and have spread the virus to many places in the United States; other species of birds are also responsible.

Different types of birds are responsible for spreading WNV in different parts of the world. Crows are one species that have been widely sickened and have spread the virus in many places, including the United States. Blue jays have also played a big role in spreading WNV in southern U.S. states. In a study reported in October 2011, biologist Marm Kilpatrick of the University of California–Santa Cruz revealed that his research indicates that robins, which most scientists thought were not widely affected by WNV, actually are "superspreaders" of WNV and that "the familiar American robin plays a key role in the transmission of West Nile virus across much of North America."[14]

Kilpatrick discovered that the reason robins are spreading WNV to such an extent is that the mosquitoes that transmit the virus seem to prefer feeding on robins over other birds in the United States. In line with these findings, other biologists have recently reported that mosquito feeding patterns, rather than the north–south migration patterns of robins and other migratory birds, have been mostly responsible for the rapid east–west spread of WNV in North America. Nonmigrating birds such as house sparrows have also been found to play a large role in spreading the virus on this continent in conjunction with mosquito feeding patterns. Researchers have discovered that mosquitoes such as *Culex tarsalis* prefer feeding on nonmigratory birds, and that these mosquitoes, which are known to travel up to 2 miles (3.24km) per day, play a significant role in spreading WNV in the United States.

The reason birds are able to spread WNV to mosquitoes that then complete the transmission cycle to humans and other animals is that the viremia, or number of virus particles, in bird blood is very high. For example, the viremia in crows and blue jays can be 1 trillion to 10 trillion viral particles per milliliter of blood. One milliliter is equivalent to about one-fifth of a teaspoon. This high viremia also explains why WNV is often fatal to these birds. In contrast, birds do not die from or spread Saint Louis encephalitis virus, because the typical viremia is about one hundred thousand virus particles per milliliter of blood.

From Birds to Mosquitoes to Other Animals

Once a bird becomes infected with WNV, the next step in the transmission cycle occurs when female mosquitoes bite the bird and later bite other animals to obtain a blood meal. Female mosquitoes bite animals because blood contains substances that help mosquito eggs develop. When a mosquito bites a bird that is infected with WNV, the virus enters the salivary glands in the mosquito's mouth. Then, when the mosquito bites another animal or person, the virus is injected into the victim's bloodstream, where it multiplies and can then migrate to the brain.

When mosquitoes become infected, however, WNV does not make them sick, even after it multiplies throughout the insect's body. Even when mosquitoes hibernate for the winter, WNV remains inside the insects but does not sicken or kill them. Then, when mosquitoes becomes active again in warmer weather, they can continue to spread the virus. This is what biologists believe happened during the winter of 1999–2000 in New York after the late summer outbreak. Hibernating, or overwintering, mosquitoes kept the virus alive during the winter months, and the following summer these mosquitoes kept spreading WNV and led to its transmission throughout the United States.

Once an infected mosquito spreads WNV to a person or animal other than a bird, the person or animal generally cannot pass the infection to anyone else, except in rare instances involving blood transfusions, organ transplants, or pregnant women and their babies. In 2004 researchers at the CDC discovered in a rare exception that alligators raised on alligator farms can pass WNV to other alligators that live in the same tank. The investigators believe this happened because the alligators developed very high viremia. Most of the time, however, humans and nonbird animals do not spread WNV. They are thus known as incidental or dead-end hosts for the virus. According to an article in *Clinical Laboratory Medicine*, "Humans (and horses) are incidental or 'dead end' hosts in this cycle because the concentration of virus within the blood

The Asian mosquito species *Aedes japonicus* was first collected in the United States in New York in 1998. A year later, the first cases of West Nile virus appeared in that region.

(viremia) is insufficient to infect a feeding naïve [uninfected] mosquito."[15]

Mosquitoes, which are necessary for transmitting the virus from the primary to the incidental host, are known as the vector of transmission. Unlike with many mosquito-borne diseases, many different kinds of mosquitoes can serve as WNV vectors. In fact, scientists have found that sixty-four mosquito species can spread the virus. The species most often responsible for spreading WNV is *Culex pipiens*. *Culex salinarius*, *Culex restuans*, *Culex tarsalis*, *Ochlerotatus canadensis*, and *Aedes vexans* are other common vectors. Different species most commonly spread WNV in different geographic regions. For example, *Culex pipiens* mostly spreads the virus in the eastern United States, and *Culex tarsalis* seems to be responsible for much of the spread in the western United States.

Culex mosquitoes bite birds, other animals, and humans, but they are most attracted to birds, which scientists say explains why they have been responsible for much of the spread of WNV. As Kilpatrick explains in a 2011 article in ScienceDaily, "The mosquitoes that bite humans most are actually not as important in transmission of West Nile virus to humans because they rarely bite birds and thus rarely get infected in the first place. Instead, it's the species that feed mostly on birds, and frequently get infected, but occasionally feed on people, that are most important."[16]

Factors That Affect the Spread of West Nile Virus

The number of infected mosquitoes in a given area, as well as the species, determines the chances of a person or animal being bitten and infected with WNV. The number of infected mosquitoes, in turn, partly depends on the number of infected birds that the mosquitoes can bite to begin the transmission cycle. The more infected birds there are, the more likely it is that many mosquitoes will become infected.

Most often, large numbers of birds are found in places near large rivers or other bodies of water, and epidemiologists have linked infected bird populations near rivers to many epidemics, including the 1996 outbreak in Romania and the 1999 outbreaks in Russia and New York. Large and small sources of standing water, as well, exacerbate the spread of WNV by giving mosquitoes places to breed. Mosquitoes often deposit their eggs in stagnant water, and the larvae then hatch and grow. In the 1996 Romanian and 1999 Russian epidemics, scientists found that standing sewage-polluted water that pooled after flooding in poorly maintained apartment basements gave *Culex pipiens* mosquitoes an opportunity to flourish, and this triggered the WNV outbreaks.

In other cases, other sources of standing water have helped mosquitoes breed in cities and rural areas where human population growth has led to the destruction of forests and other natural habitats. When forests are destroyed to obtain wood for houses or to clear areas for growing food, this leaves more areas where standing water can settle. Animal habitats also disappear, and this leads to disruptions in the balance of animal and insect life that can favor mosquito population growth because mosquito predators die off. When wetlands, which consist of areas around oceans, lakes, and rivers, are destroyed by humans, this, too, can increase mosquito populations. As Thomas Baptist of the National Audubon Society explains in the book *West Nile Virus*:

> In many cases, mosquito problems are the result of human impacts on our wetland systems, and restoring wetlands and waterways to a more natural condition can help restore Nature's own mosquito control processes. For example, in a healthy tidal wetland system, fish eat large numbers of mosquitoes and their larvae, helping to control insect populations. Wherever tidal flow has been restricted or wetlands have been dammed, ditched, filled or otherwise impacted, this natural balance may be disrupted.[17]

Many scientists believe mosquito populations have also increased worldwide because of global climate change. They suggest that global climate change has led to more extreme weather patterns, such as heavy rains, which can leave standing water where mosquitoes breed.

Climate Change, Global Expansion, and the Spread of WNV

Warmer outdoor temperatures increase both mosquito breeding and activity, and this is why these creatures thrive in summer and hibernate in winter. It is also why most WNV infections occur during the summer months. Overall warming temperatures also give mosquitoes an opportunity to breed and bite people and animals during multiple seasons, and higher temperatures can affect the speed and amount of transmission of WNV from mosquitoes to people and animals. An article in *Smithsonian* magazine explains:

If the temperature outdoors is 70 degrees Fahrenheit, it takes more than three weeks for West Nile virus to multiply throughout the body of a northern house mosquito, and only 10 percent of the mosquitoes will be able to transmit the virus. At 80 degrees F, the virus multiplies in two weeks, and 20 to 25 percent of the insects are infectious. But when the temperature goes to 90 degrees F, it takes only a week for the virus to multiply—and about 75 percent of the insects can transmit disease.[18]

A lab technician examines a dead blue jay suspected of carrying West Nile virus. Birds have been the primary way West Nile virus has spread.

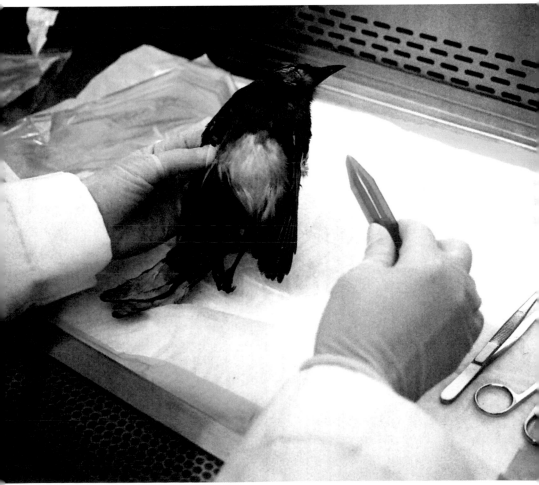

West Nile Virus Spread and Global Climate Change

Many scientists believe global climate change is contributing to the increasing spread of new diseases, including WNV, around the world. Paul R. Epstein of the Harvard Medical School told U.S. government officials:

The means by which the virus causing mosquito-borne encephalitis entered the New York region in the fall of 1999 are not known. But the climatic conditions favoring diseases that cycle among birds, urban mosquitoes and humans are well understood, and there are important lessons to be drawn from this emerging disease and its association with climate variability and change . . . . Mild winters and summer dry spells favor breeding of city-dwelling mosquitoes (*Culex pipiens*), while extended droughts kill off their predators. The prolonged July heat wave may have amplified the virus maturation and circulation among mosquitoes and congregating birds, while late August rains unleashed a new crop of Aedes mosquitoes that may have acted as an additional "bridge" vector to humans.

Quoted in US Senate Subcommittee on Environment and Public Works. *West Nile Virus.* Washington, DC: US Government Printing Office, 2000, pp. 49–50.

Many scientists have suggested that increased worldwide temperatures and the subsequent expansion of the number of days in which mosquitoes are actively breeding may also explain why diseases such as WNV have recently spread to areas where they had never before appeared. A report of the Intergovernmental Panel on Climate Change states, "Indirect effects of climate change include increases in the potential transmission of vector-borne infectious diseases, for instance, malaria, yellow fever, and some viral encephalitis, resulting from extensions of the geographical range and season for vector organisms."[19]

Warming temperatures can also impact the replication speed of WNV and thus contribute to the virus's increasing spread throughout the world. In a 2009 article in *PLoS Pathogens*, researcher Michael S. Diamond of Washington University in St. Louis explains that a mutation in the virus in 2002 changed one amino acid and enhanced the ability of the virus to replicate at higher temperatures. This in turn allowed the rapid spread of the virus among birds in the United States. Diamond writes, "Thus, a single amino acid change on WNV has led to rapid geographic expansion and increased intensity of transmission."[20]

Biologist Theodore Andreadis of the Connecticut Department of Soil and Water pointed out to a U.S. congressional committee in 1999 that another factor besides global climate change—increased global movement—is also fueling the spread of WNV and may in fact be of even more concern to public health officials. *Global movement* refers to the movement of people, animals, and cargo from one region of the world to another. Andreadis said, "I think a more important issue [in the spread of WNV] is the global movement of organisms, and I think this is a greater threat than global warming to the introduction of an exotic virus or new disease. We have a global economy. We have global movement. You can be in Europe today and in Asia tomorrow."[21] Many experts believe that foreign cargo, animals, or people coming to the United States in 1999 were responsible for starting the WNV epidemic in New York, since this was the first incident in this part of the world.

Other Modes of Transmission

Whatever the environmental factors that have promoted the spread of WNV may be, the introduction of the virus into the United States brought other, previously unknown modes of transmission to light. Epidemiologists used to think that mosquitoes were the only means by which WNV could be spread from birds to other animals and people, but starting in 2002 instances of people contracting WNV from blood transfusions or organ transplants were reported. In the first reported cases, four people who received organs from an infected donor who

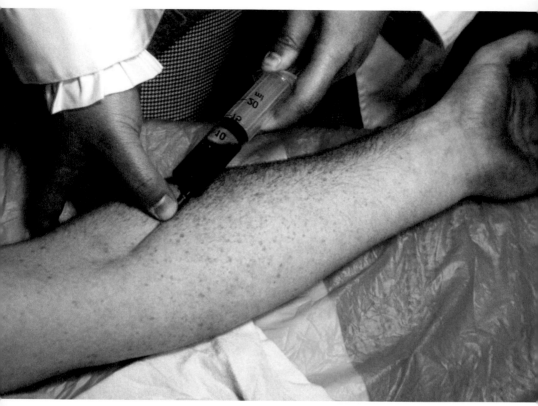

In 2002 it was discovered that people were contracting West Nile virus from blood transfusions and organ transplants.

died in a car accident in Georgia developed symptoms of WNV two weeks after their operations. A woman who received a kidney transplant developed fever, diarrhea, a rash, back pain, and breathing difficulties. She had to be placed on a ventilator to breathe but eventually recovered. A man who received the donor's other kidney developed similar symptoms and died. Tests revealed that all four patients had identical strains of WNV.

Reports of people developing WNV after blood transfusions also surfaced, and doctors were surprised because no cases involving this type of transmission had ever been reported elsewhere in the world. However, as Jesse Goodman of the U.S. Food and Drug Administration (FDA) states in the book *Responding to the Public Health Threat of West Nile Virus*:

We knew that such transmission was plausible because the virus is believed to be present in the blood for a period of a couple of days to weeks early in infection, including in patients who never develop symptoms of infection. Thus, a donor could feel well but, after mosquito exposure, could have the virus present in the blood for a short time and while unaware of this, could donate blood. However, the risk of such an infected donor transmitting infection was believed to be very low.[22]

Despite this low risk, once cases of transfusion and organ transplant transmission of WNV came to light, health experts became alarmed, in part because people who receive these treatments are often very ill and are more likely to develop severe neuroinvasive WNV. Widespread screening of blood and organ donors for WNV began. Screening involves asking potential donors whether they have any symptoms of illness, as well as testing their blood and tissues for the virus with laboratory tests that detect WNV genetic material.

Other Nonmosquito Transmission

In addition to finding out that WNV can be spread through infected blood or organs, doctors have discovered that sometimes the virus is spread by other means as well. Two such means of transmission are from a pregnant woman to her fetus and from a nursing mother to her baby, though this happens very rarely. The first instance of transmission from a pregnant woman to her fetus occurred in New York in 2002, when a pregnant woman developed a fever, headache, vomiting, and back and abdominal pain. Tests revealed that she had WNV. Her baby was born three months later with severe birth defects and antibodies to WNV in its blood. Doctors concluded that the mother infected the baby and that the virus possibly caused the birth defects.

Instances of laboratory workers being infected after they were accidentally stabbed with contaminated needles or scalpels have also occurred. In one case a microbiologist was removing a dead bird's brain with a scalpel and cut his thumb.

Laboratory Biosafety and West Nile Virus

After several laboratory workers became infected with WNV after being wounded with infected needles or scalpels, the CDC changed the biosafety rules for laboratories handling the virus. WNV now requires BSL3 precautions, which include that laboratory personnel receive special safety training and that they be supervised by specially trained scientists. According to the CDC, some of the other BSL3 requirements are:

- Needles and other sharp objects must be carefully handled and disposed of.
- All work surfaces must be decontaminated with disinfectant after work is completed.
- Anything containing viruses must be decontaminated before it is disposed of.
- Workers must do any work with infectious materials inside a biosafety container.
- Workers must wear protective clothing and equipment, including gowns, goggles, masks, and gloves.
- People may enter the laboratory only through two self-closing doors. The ventilation system can only take air from clean to potentially contaminated areas.

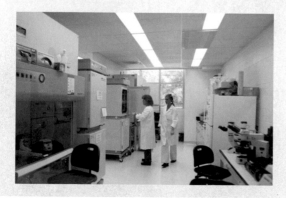

The University of Georgia's Animal Health Research Center is one of only a few in the world with a biosafety level 3 rating.

He thoroughly cleaned and bandaged the wound, but four days later he developed symptoms of WNV infection. Blood tests revealed that he had been infected with the same viral strain that the bird had.

After several such incidents, the CDC, National Institutes of Health, and U.S. Department of Health and Human Services issued strict guidelines for laboratories working with WNV. Laboratories that handle pathogens must comply with regulations set forth by these agencies to protect workers and to ensure that infectious agents do not get out of these facilities. These agencies classify hazardous germs according to how dangerous they are, using a biosafety scale ranging from biosafety level 1 to biosafety level 4. Level 4 applies to the most dangerous pathogens. WNV is classified as a biosafety level 3 (BSL3) agent. Methods of containment (proper handling and protection) for BSL3 agents include detailed measures to prevent people from touching or inhaling the pathogen and other protocols to confine it to special enclosed containers.

Despite these instances of people contracting WNV from laboratory accidents, blood transfusions, organ transplants, or mother-to-baby transmission, public health experts emphasize that the virus is very rarely spread in these ways. In addition, WNV has never, to anyone's knowledge, been spread by casual contact or by being near an infected person or animal. The usual method of transmission, by mosquito bites, is by far the most likely method of becoming infected, and educating the public about the spread of WNV centers on this fact.

CHAPTER THREE

Treatment for and Living with West Nile Virus

One reason medical experts are so concerned about the rapid spread of WNV is that there are not yet any treatments that cure or combat the disease. According to the CDC:

> There is no specific treatment for WNV infection. In cases with milder symptoms, people experience symptoms such as fever and aches that pass on their own, although even healthy people have become sick for several weeks. In more severe cases, people usually need to go to the hospital, where they receive supportive treatment including intravenous fluids, help with breathing and nursing care.[23]

Supportive treatments involve making a patient as comfortable as possible until the immune system can fight off the infection. Patients with mild disease are advised to drink plenty of fluids to prevent dehydration, to get plenty of rest, and to take fever- and pain-reducing medications such as aspirin or acetaminophen if needed. For those who are hospitalized with severe illness, supportive treatment may also involve administering drugs to reduce swelling in the brain or to diminish seizures. If a patient cannot eat, he or she may need to have fluids administered through an intravenous tube and food through a feeding tube inserted into the stomach. If a patient cannot breathe, he or she would need ventilator support.

Antiviral Drugs

Despite the availability of drugs that treat general symptoms such as fevers and aches, doctors have thus far not found any medications that specifically treat WNV infections. Doctors originally believed that the antiviral drug ribavirin might be helpful, since several studies showed that it killed WNV in a test tube, and other research indicated it was effective in treating yellow fever and Japanese encephalitis virus, which are caused by flaviviruses similar to WNV. Despite these promising results, studies on mice and human patients have shown ribavirin to be ineffective and in some cases even to worsen symptoms.

Doctors are hopeful that other antiviral drugs such as interferons (IFNs), which are synthetic versions of naturally occurring immune chemicals, may prove to be effective against WNV. Immune cells naturally produce several types of IFNs after a virus is recognized in the body as a foreign protein. Interferons stimulate the body's immune response to the viral infection. Interferons alpha, beta, and gamma are the most-studied types of IFN.

Doctors are able to successfully treat some infectious diseases with synthetic IFNs, and several studies have tested these substances against WNV with mixed results. Treating WNV-infected cells in laboratory cultures with IFN-alpha and beta weakens the virus and inhibits its ability to replicate, but only when the drugs are administered before the virus begins replicating. Scientists at Washington University School of Medicine concluded that "in vitro [in a test tube], WNV has been shown to be acutely sensitive to IFNs when cells are treated prior to infection, but like other flaviviruses, this sensitivity is largely lost when cells are treated after WNV infection is established."[24] Whether this means that IFNs will be effective in treating patients if administered before the virus replicates remains to be seen.

Despite these results, some researchers have explored the benefits of using IFN treatments with WNV patients in various stages of illness. Some studies have shown that mice that do not produce IFNs become extremely ill and die from WNV, and

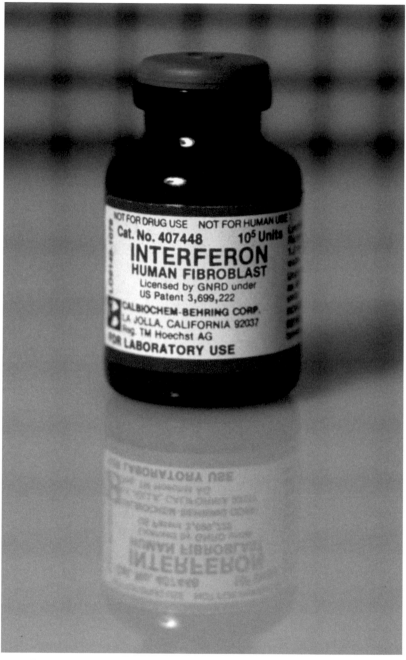

Interferon, a protein produced by the body in response to viral infection, has been synthesized and used as a drug to fight West Nile virus.

these findings led researchers to believe that IFNs might be helpful in treating people with WNV. In 2005 researchers at the University of Nebraska Medical Center in Omaha gave IFN-alpha injections to two severely ill WNV patients and found that the drug helped them recover. In 2007 a patient who received IFN-alpha three weeks after he became infected recovered, indicating that the drug had an effect on already-replicating viruses. Positive results have also been achieved in horses. Other attempts to use IFN-alpha or -beta against WNV have not been promising, however, because these substances have not helped infected people in several subsequent studies.

Despite these mixed results, doctors believe IFNs warrant further testing against WNV, and clinical trials have begun with Intron A, a form of IFN-alpha now approved to treat hepatitis C. The drug has serious side effects, such as fever and pain, and it can prevent bone marrow from producing blood cells, but doctors say it may be effective in saving the lives of severely ill WNV patients.

Psychological Effects of West Nile Virus

Until a treatment such as IFN or another medication proves effective against WNV, supportive treatments are all that are available. This fact, along with the discomfort and disability that goes along with moderate or severe WNV illness, contributes to making life with the disease physically and psychologically challenging. For many patients, the lack of a viable therapy is among the most disheartening aspects of living with WNV. A patient named Chris Cottrell was out of work for four months as he struggled with headaches, fatigue, tremors, and numbness. According to an Oshkosh, Wisconsin, newspaper article, "Cottrell found the inability to treat the virus the most frustrating. . . . While he sat at home, battling intense headaches and losing weight—30 pounds in all—doctors were unable to help, except to treat his symptoms. At one point, he said, he was taking pain relievers, including the occasional Vicodin, every two hours to relieve the aches."[25]

For sixteen-year-old Caidey, who developed severe WNV encephalitis in 2010 and has had lingering effects, the lack of treatment is also discouraging and worrisome. Caidey writes on the Encephalitis Global Support Community website that dealing with continuous pain, dizziness, and nausea has worn her down physically and emotionally, in part because, as she states, "my doctors pretty much told me that they don't know why I am left with these conditions, they will never know, and there is no way to treat them, that I am stuck with these conditions for the rest of my life . . . all they do is treat my pain with

One Patient's Experience

For Richard Lyon of California, living with West Nile encephalitis and its aftermath was a nearly fatal and life-changing ordeal. Lyon experienced one complication after another for nearly a year after being infected on a camping trip in September 2005 and wrote about his experience in an article titled "My West Nile Story." Especially frightening, he wrote, was the mental confusion that hospital nurses later described to him: "Nurses would ask me simple questions like 'what was my name'? I'd take twenty minutes trying to figure it out and respond. I was told that I was asked if I knew where I was at and I responded 'Wal Mart.'"

A few weeks later, while in a rehabilitation hospital relearning how to walk, he developed severe chest pains and was rushed back to a regular hospital. Doctors could find nothing wrong, so he was sent to another hospital, then back to rehabilitation, then home. Once home, he experienced tremors, severe stomach pain and vomiting, and more chest pain. This time doctors at the hospital discovered he had blood clots in his lungs from inactivity during his previous hospitalizations. He also had a large mass in his stomach and had to have part of his stomach removed. After he went home, he developed PTSD from the emotional stress. This complication later resolved itself, but Lyon was left with permanent vision, hearing, and nerve damage. Still, he wrote, "Boy it's great to be alive!"

Richard Lyon. "My West Nile Story." Yahoo! Voices, April 9, 2008. http://voices.yahoo
.com/my-west-nile-story-1350609.html.

heavy narcotics." In addition, every time she gets something as minor as a cold, "it is almost like the virus re-activates and I go through everything all over again,"[26] she says. For patients such as Caidey, it can feel as if there is no positive end in sight to the suffering caused by WNV.

Other patients may struggle most with the life-changing effects that can possibly result from a WNV infection, such as lingering symptoms or permanent disability. Living with memory loss; vision, speech, and hearing problems; or paralysis, weakness, or muscle control problems can be emotionally as well as physically devastating, and many people with temporary or chronic disability require mental health counseling or antidepressant drugs to help them cope with their changed lives and with the need to keep going for physical rehabilitation therapies that may or may not help.

Richard Lyon endured multiple hospitalizations for many months due to West Nile encephalitis and various complications, including chest pains, blood clots in his lungs, and stomach blockages that required the removal of part of his stomach. As a result of these experiences, he developed post-traumatic stress disorder (PTSD). This is a mental condition in which people who have experienced traumatic events keep flashing back to those events and panicking. Lyon eventually recovered from PTSD, but lasting numbness, weakness, vision and hearing problems, and other complications meant that life as he once knew it would not return.

Like Lyon, many patients with lasting disability find that their lives are never the same as they were before WNV. Ken Speake, a TV news reporter in Minnesota, had to retire from his job four years after becoming infected. Having to give up a career he loved was extremely difficult, as he wrote in 2007:

> I've struggled with fatigue since West Nile virus knocked me off my feet for two months in the fall of 2003. I'm just so tired. There are times I want to cry. It's the mental work at the word processor that is energy expensive for me now. In January of 2006, I began working four days a week. Wednesdays, I sleep. It helps. But the fatigue piles up. . . .

Kinda snowballs, if you will. I'm confused and angered that I don't have the vigor I want to have. I remember being vigorous. So, I'm going to retire.[27]

Long-Term Effects

The lasting effects of WNV can change different people's lives to varying degrees, depending on how severe and long-lasting the effects are. A study reported in 2008 in ScienceDaily revealed that "persistent symptoms of West Nile infection still plagued 60% of patients in the study at the end of the first year."[28] Forty percent of the patients in the study still had memory loss, tremors, and loss of balance five years after infection, and many experienced persistent depression as well. One of the researchers, Kristy Murray of the University of Texas Health Science Center in Houston, explained that the study also found that most recovery occurred within two years after infection: "Once they hit two years it completely plateaus. If a patient has not recovered by that time, it is very likely they will never recover."[29] Subsequent studies showed that some patients still had persistent symptoms and disability ten years after infection. Those who initially had West Nile encephalitis are most likely to have these long-term effects, but those who had other types of neuroinvasive disease are often affected as well. The longer any symptoms or disabilities persist, the more likely these conditions are to contribute to long-term coping challenges and adjustments.

Doctors find that people with persistent symptoms who do improve often do so because they force themselves to continue with intensive rehabilitation therapies, which may include physical, occupational, and speech therapy. Physical therapy is administered by a licensed physical therapist, who stimulates muscles and prescribes exercises to help strengthen and retrain muscles to move after they have been weakened by paralysis or simply from the person being bedridden for a long time. Some patients must learn to walk again, and many require occupational therapy, in which occupational therapists help them relearn or develop new ways of performing everyday tasks like

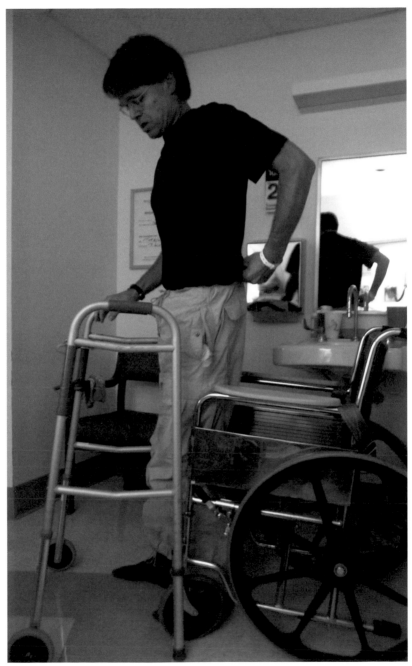

A West Nile virus patient paralyzed by the virus uses a walker to move around his hospital room. Sixty percent of West Nile victims still have persistent symptoms of infection after a year.

eating, dressing, and bathing. Speech therapists help patients relearn how to speak or swallow if patients lost these skills when muscles or brain centers that control these functions were paralyzed or otherwise damaged.

After Melissa Dimond of Utah spent a month in the hospital with West Nile meningoencephalitis, she remained unable to do simple things like swallow, smile, or walk. She also had serious memory problems; for example, she could not remember how to use the insulin pump she needed to treat her type 1 diabetes. She began extensive rehabilitation therapy to relearn literally everything she once knew—even how to cough—and stuck with the therapies despite constant setbacks and frustrations. Two years later Dimond still had trouble walking and tired easily, but she was able to return to her job as a state epidemiologist.

Some patients, however, never regain all or most of their previous abilities despite months or years of dedicated efforts. Even after a year of rehabilitation therapy, Richard Gibson of Saskatchewan, Canada, was not able to return to his job as a minister. Doctors were initially unsure of whether Gibson would live when severe WNV meningitis left him paralyzed in 2007. By 2008 he could walk with a walker and use his right arm, but his left arm remained paralyzed. Gibson and his wife channeled his struggles into organizing a support group for WNV survivors so they could share their experiences. In a West Nile Virus Survivors Foundation story, Gibson said, "I'm far beyond what anyone thought possible, but I'm nowhere near where I was. . . . Most people don't recognize how serious it [WNV] can be."[30]

Some patients with lingering disability that has not been helped by most rehabilitation therapies have benefited from electrical stimulation devices such as the Ness L300. Manufactured by Bioness, this device has a leg cuff that fits below the knee, a sensor, and a wireless communicator that lets the sensor and electrical stimulator communicate. The device can be attached to a leg brace to stimulate muscles under the brace, but it forces the muscles, rather than the brace, to do the work. When the Ness L300 is turned on, an electric current activates

A physical therapist helps a patient use the Ness L300 leg cuffs to walk. The device electronically stimulates the muscles to work in those who are paralyzed, including those paralyzed from West Nile virus infection.

nerves and muscles to help a person lift his or her foot. This device helped Elizabeth Zopff of Colorado lift her foot after WNV paralyzed her right leg. She had struggled to walk with a cane and leg brace for two years but could not lift her right foot until she started using the Ness L300.

Impact on Families

In addition to changing some patients' lives by leaving them with varying degrees of disability, severe WNV infections also impact the families of these patients. The emotional and financial toll of having a loved one hospitalized and needing rehabilitation can be serious and is often worsened when the ill individual cannot work temporarily or permanently. Mel Lacy of Idaho, for example, had medical insurance, but the insurance carrier dropped him after paying out over $750,000 for his hospital care. Even when he still had the insurance, his co-payments and deductibles cost his family thousands of dollars

Effects from severe West Nile infections can last for years and seriously impact patients' families emotionally and financially.

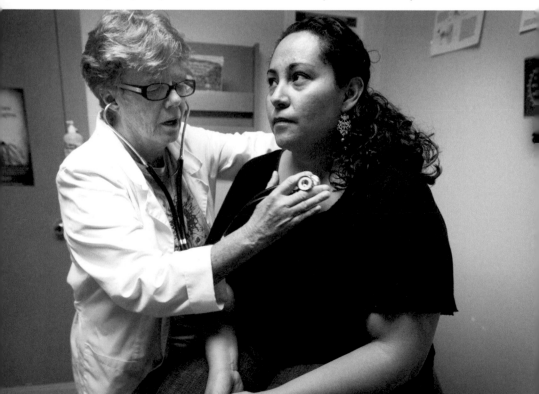

out of pocket. A family member who must constantly be at the hospital with a seriously ill person or who must care for the patient at home may also have to stop working, and this can worsen the family's financial situation.

When twenty-two-year-old Daniel Williams of Tallahassee, Florida, developed severe West Nile meningoencephalitis in 2011, the financial strain for his retired parents was substantial. His parents were financially stable but had little in savings, and paying the 20 percent copayments for Daniel's hospital care after their insurance paid 80 percent soon became a huge concern. The first of many bills they received was for $326,000. Daniel's mother, Mimi, said in an article that caring for Daniel had to be their first priority, so "we can't go back to work, because we need to be there for Daniel and each other."[31]

As in the Williams case, coping with the practical and emotional challenges of WNV disease can be especially difficult when the ill person is a child or young adult. In part this is because severe WNV disease is so rare in young people and is therefore unexpected. In addition, seeing one's child suffer through an illness or death is emotionally devastating for a parent. When her son David, a graduate student at Clemson University in South Carolina, became very sick in 2007, Gayle Kelly said in a newspaper article, "I always thought that West Nile virus was something other people got. Certainly not my son."[32] When emergency room doctors initially diagnosed David with pneumonia and sent him home, Gayle's instincts told her the problem was much more serious, and she took her son back to the hospital and demanded that he be properly diagnosed. Doctors later told her that her instincts saved David's life, because when he developed seizures and heart problems from the WNV infection after returning to the hospital, physicians were able to administer lifesaving treatments quickly. David eventually recovered and after extensive rehabilitation therapy was able to walk again.

Some young people, however, die from severe WNV illness, as happened with seventeen-year-old Lauren Ashley Miller of Canada in 2008, four years after she was infected. Encephalitis left Lauren in a vegetative state, and her parents took her to

China to receive an experimental stem cell injection not available anywhere else because it had not been proved to be safe or effective. The Millers claimed that the injection improved Lauren's ability to swallow. They then tried hyperbaric oxygen treatments, which involve placing a patient in a special chamber that floods the body with highly concentrated oxygen. Hyperbaric oxygen treatments can improve circulation and brain function in some cases, but Lauren died despite these measures.

Maintaining Hope

Trying alternative, unproven remedies like those the Millers sought for their daughter is just one of the many things that desperate patients and their families do to maintain hope in the face of a life-threatening disease for which no viable treatments exist. Some people try other alternative remedies, including special diets, herbal concoctions such as biscuit root, or massive doses of vitamin C, though medical experts stress that none has been proved to be effective, because these options offer hope that conventional medicine cannot offer in cases of severe WNV illness.

Many people assert that maintaining hope is critical in giving them the strength and willpower to forge ahead in a difficult situation, and trying alternative remedies is not the only way in which people maintain their hope. Different patients and families derive hope from different sources. For many patients, hope comes from loved ones staying close and refusing to give up. Others find that their religious beliefs sustain their hope and strength. For Mel Lacy, who survived being paralyzed and not being able to breathe on his own, his strong religious faith helped spur his determination not to give up as he continued with extensive physical therapy. Lacy writes, "I had cancer at age 34 that they said I wouldn't live through (it), and I thought I had done my hard part in life and I passed those odds and then when I got this [WNV] I thought well, there's really a challenge. . . . They do have antidepressants to help. But I really believe its my faith that gets me by where I am."[33]

Because many people are unaware of how devastating severe WNV illness can be, many patients and families also find

Alternative Treatments for West Nile Virus

Because of the lack of viable treatments for WNV illness, many patients try alternative therapies to alleviate debilitating symptoms. Alternative practitioners commonly recommend herbal or vitamin supplements, which are not regulated by the FDA the way drugs are. Medical doctors point out that these substances can contain toxins and can interact adversely with any medications a person is taking. Herbal and supplement manufacturers also frequently make unfounded claims about product effectiveness, even though none has proved to be safe or effective for treating WNV. For example, an alternative medicine website promoting the use of vitamin C to cure WNV infection states, "It has been proven that massive doses of sodium ascorbate [vitamin C] intravenously can cure West Nile."[1] No scientific studies, however, have proved this claim, and doctors caution people to be wary. In commenting on studies that show that many people take unproven remedies, Arshad Jahangir of the Mayo Clinic states in a Medpage Today article, "The surprise for me was . . . how much people are willing to spend on a type of therapy which has not shown, in any scientific way, to be effective or safe."[2] In the same article, David Meyers of Johns Hopkins University says, "It's unfortunately very big business, and potential drug interactions and potential harmful effects abound."[3]

1. Robert F. Cathcart. "West Nile Virus." Orthomed.com. www.orthomed.com/Nile.htm.
2. Quoted in John Gever. "Hidden Dangers of Herbal Meds Reviewed." MedPage Today, February 1, 2010. www.medpagetoday.com/PrimaryCare/AlternativeMedicine/18244.
3. Quoted in Gever. "Hidden Dangers of Herbal Meds Reviewed."

that they derive hope from educating the public about the dangers of WNV and about ways of preventing infection. In this way they derive satisfaction from knowing they have possibly prevented someone else from enduring the ordeal with which they are so familiar. Utah epidemiologist Melissa Dimond and her husband, for example, speak out frequently about the importance of preventive measures, ever since Melissa spent six months relearning how to do everything, including swallowing and walking, after West Nile meningoencephalitis robbed her of these abilities. Richard Lyon, who was in and out of the hospital for nearly a year with complications from WNV, also encourages others to do all they can to prevent infection. As he writes, "Never underestimate the power of one mosquito."[34]

CHAPTER FOUR

Prevention and Control

Because there are no specific treatments for WNV disease, public health officials are focused on trying to prevent the incidence and spread of the virus. Prevention is also emphasized because the 1999 WNV epidemic in New York took public health agencies by surprise and revealed many areas where preventive measures might have protected the United States from the West Nile invasion. As Durland Fish, a professor of epidemiology at Yale University, told a U.S. Senate subcommittee, "We were woefully ill-prepared for this epidemic of West Nile virus . . . [but] these events, as shocking as they may seem to the general public, were actually predicted and warned by the scientific community. Two reports from the National Academy of Sciences warned of a decaying public health infrastructure, particularly in reference to insect-borne diseases."[35]

Congress, however, did not act on these warnings prior to 1999, and many experts believe this lack of planning for an incursion of a new virus into the United States allowed the epidemic to sicken and kill many Americans. The lack of planning also led public health officials in New York to order the massive aerial spraying of insecticides once they determined that mosquitoes were spreading WNV. This exposed about 10 million people and millions more animals to potentially dangerous chemicals. Being prepared with preventive strategies, states Fish, would have allowed the use of less toxic methods

After the West Nile epidemic in New York, the state sprayed massive amount of insecticides, exposing 10 million people to potentially dangerous chemicals that critics say could have been avoided with better planning and prevention.

of controlling the spread of the virus. Because of these short-comings in the 1999 response, emphasizing a proactive rather than an after-the-fact approach to WNV control has become the overriding objective in the United States.

Past experiences with other arboviruses, Fish emphasizes, show that prevention programs like the one he is proposing can work. "Epidemics of insect-borne disease are preventable. We have eliminated the threat of epidemic malaria, yellow fever, and bubonic plague in this country years ago, but we have left our guard down against the threat of new diseases, such as West Nile virus,"[36] he states. To address public health deficiencies that have allowed WNV to spread throughout the United States, officials have developed and put in place prevention and control programs they hope will reduce further spread and impact.

Coordination and Mobilization

Part of implementing national strategies for preventing and controlling WNV involves mobilizing and coordinating local, state, and federal agencies. The CDC's Division of Vector-Borne Diseases, the U.S. Department of Agriculture, and the U.S. Geological Survey's National Wildlife Health Center have taken the lead in formulating action plans. These plans include guidelines for sharing information, tracking the disease, and coordinating resources throughout the nation.

A wide range of specialists, including arbovirologists (experts in insect-borne diseases), epidemiologists, mosquito control experts, microbiologists, veterinarians, physicians, and laboratory technicians have been called upon to help formulate and execute these plans. The CDC's ArboNET monitoring system coordinates ongoing communication between experts and agencies to allow quick responses to signs of outbreaks in an effort to prevent WNV from spreading.

In issuing guidelines for monitoring the spread of WNV, CDC officials note that reporting of suspicious local events by medical professionals and the general public is the foundation on which any national plan must build. Local agencies are most likely to recognize early signs of an epidemic as they receive reports of bird, animal, and human illnesses and deaths. As the book *West Nile Virus Outbreak* explains:

> The potential that one or two persons' medical conditions could be an indication of some larger concern, such as an emerging infectious disease, may not be readily apparent to the health professionals involved. In many cases, such events might not be noticed until a number of physicians have reported the cases and the local health department identifies a cluster, or a number of victims seek care for

similar conditions at the same location. Alert responses by the doctors and nurses who first see such victims are particularly crucial in alerting the public health community to the possibility of a wider problem.[37]

CDC director Dr. Julie Gerberding provides an update on West Nile virus in California in 2004. Implementing a national strategy against West Nile involves mobilizing and coordinating local, state, and federal agencies.

Incidences of West Nile Virus in the United States Reported by ArboNET as of September 4, 2012

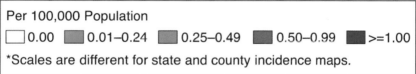

Per 100,000 Population

☐ 0.00 ◼ 0.01–0.24 ◼ 0.25–0.49 ◼ 0.50–0.99 ◼ >=1.00

*Scales are different for state and county incidence maps.

Taken from: Centers for Disease Control and Prevention. www.cdc.gov.

Surveillance

Once a problem is detected, local surveillance (monitoring) and mosquito control efforts can then be increased to stem the spread of the virus. Local surveillance of infected birds, mosquitoes, animals, and people is one of the most critical elements in beginning effective WNV control measures. The CDC states, "Appropriate and timely response to surveillance data is key to preventing human and animal disease. . . . That response must include effective mosquito control and public education without delay, if an increasing intensity of virus activity is detected."[38] This type of response to surveillance data makes people aware of what they can do to protect themselves, while also reducing mosquito populations to cut down on disease spread.

West Nile Virus and Bioterrorism

The issue of bioterrorism has arisen in discussions of public health preparedness and prevention of the spread of WNV in the United States. Bioterrorism involves terrorists releasing dangerous viruses or bacteria to kill people. Public health experts do not believe the introduction of WNV into the United States in 1999 was an act of bioterrorism. According to the book *West Nile Virus Outbreak*, however, "Although the outbreak is considered to have been a natural occurrence—possibly introduced by international travelers, migrating birds, or mosquitoes accidentally brought from abroad—it can also provide lessons about detecting and responding to an act of biological terrorism."

Bioterrorism experts do not consider an attack using WNV to be likely, because the virus is not spread from person to person through the air or through casual contact. However, they still emphasize that when doctors and other health experts remain alert for and report "natural" outbreaks of illnesses like WNV disease, this also helps the government prepare for and defend citizens against bioterrorist attacks. "Because a bioterrorist event could look like a natural outbreak, bioterrorism preparedness rests in large part on public health preparedness," states the book *West Nile Virus Outbreak*.

U.S. General Accounting Office/Health, Education, and Human Services Division. *West Nile Virus Outbreak: Lessons for Public Health Preparedness*. Washington, DC: U.S. General Accounting Office, 2000, p. 3, 5.

Although surveillance and control measures were not adequate in New York City in 1999, neighboring Connecticut had effective programs in place, and these programs did much to prevent the degree of virus spread that occurred in New York. Public health officials in Connecticut implemented an ongoing mosquito and bird surveillance program in 1997 to halt the spread of a mosquito-borne illness called eastern equine encephalitis. Although Connecticut's program did not entirely prevent WNV from entering the state, according to a report by Theodore Andreadis of the Connecticut Department of Soil and Water, "[Connecticut's] timely, coordinated response in trapping and testing mosquitoes and birds provided indispensable data that was effectively used to inform and protect the public."[39] Many of the current surveillance and prevention programs throughout the United States are modeled on the Connecticut measures.

Surveillance programs use birds and other animals, especially horses, which are frequently bitten by mosquitoes, as

Disease surveillance begins with collecting samples of mosquitoes to check them for the West Nile virus.

sentinels, or warning flags, of increased disease activity. Veterinarians and horse owners have been encouraged to report illness or death in horses, and the general public in various locales also reports bird deaths to local public health agencies to help with tracking WNV. Biologists then take blood or tissue samples from sick or dead animals to assess whether WNV is present. One problem with bird surveillance is that since wild birds can travel long distances, the place where they are found dead may not be where they became infected. Biologists thus use domestic birds such as chickens as sentinels of WNV activity in a particular area as well.

Ongoing surveillance of mosquitoes is also performed, and if animal sentinels indicate increased WNV activity in a particular area, the mosquito surveillance is intensified. Mosquito surveillance begins with using different types of traps to collect and identify the insects. Light traps are most often used. These contraptions use light to attract mosquitoes and also contain a small motor, fan, and battery-powered photocell connected to the light. The photocell detects daylight and turns the trap's light on at dusk and off at daybreak. When mosquitoes enter the trap, the fan blows them into a collection jar. A variation on this type of trap uses propane gas, rather than batteries, for power.

Though light traps are most common, there are other options available. Another type of trap, the carbon dioxide–baited light trap, uses dry ice (carbon dioxide) to attract mosquitoes. Carbon dioxide is the gas breathed out by people and animals, and it is what attracts mosquitoes to living creatures. A third type of trap is the gravid or oviposition trap containing hay or manure, which attracts gravid female mosquitoes (*gravid* means ready to release their eggs). The trap is connected to a suction device that pulls the insects into a collection box. Some traps target certain species of mosquitoes. For example, Fay Prince traps have contrasting black and white panels, plus carbon dioxide, to attract mosquitoes that are active during the day.

Once mosquitoes are trapped, biologists count them and determine the percentage that are infected with WNV. They then calculate the infection rate, which is the estimated number of infected mosquitoes per one thousand mosquitoes tested. When infection rates reach a certain state-determined level, emergency insecticide-spraying measures begin, which aim to destroy mosquitoes so human and animal infections can be prevented or curtailed. The goal of ongoing mosquito surveillance and control, however, is to use safer, nonemergency methods of killing mosquitoes before the more dangerous emergency measures are required.

Mosquito Control

Mosquito eradication efforts can target any of the four stages of mosquito development—the egg, larva, pupa, or mature adult. Females lay their eggs in standing water, and after about two days the eggs hatch and larvae emerge. One to two weeks later, the larvae develop into pupae, and one to four days later, a mature mosquito flies away. Since females can lay eggs every ten to fourteen days, mosquito populations can increase rapidly.

Public health officials prefer to target the first three stages of growth because the immature insects can be more carefully targeted than flying adults. One method of killing eggs, larvae, and pupae involves draining standing water or marshes where these immature creatures grow. Without water the young mosquitoes will die. An alternative method involves changing breeding areas, such as marshes, by either flooding them or digging ditches to help them drain. Introducing larva-eating fish such as gambusia into breeding areas can also be effective. A final option is applying larvicides directly onto breeding sites. Larvicides, or chemicals tthat kill larvae, can be sprinkled rather than sprayed, which is much safer for humans and animals since the chemicals do not become airborne. However, if animals drink the water where the chemicals are applied, they can die.

Once immature mosquitoes become adults, the most common method of killing them is spraying insecticides from trucks or airplanes. Ground-based spraying is more closely targeted and is thus considered to be safer for people and animals than aerial spraying, but aerial spraying covers more area. Beyond the safety concerns over these chemicals, mosquitoes also tend to develop resistance to insecticides. When this happens, stronger, more

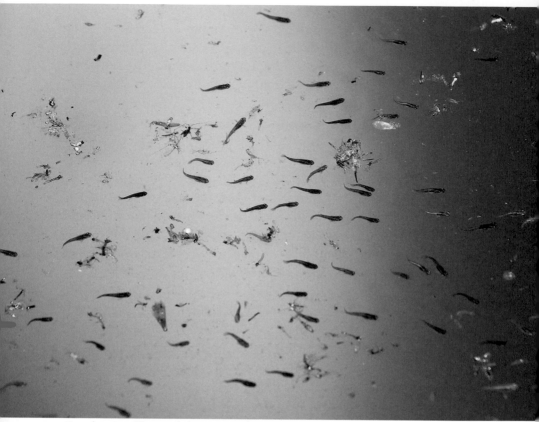

Gambusia affinis, a fish species that eats mosquito larvae, has been effectively used to control mosquitoes by introducing the fish into waters where mosquitoes breed.

toxic formulations are needed to kill the insects, and these substances are also more dangerous to people and animals.

After the massive air-based spraying of the insecticide malathion in 1999 in New York City, public health officials determined that future prevention and control efforts should focus on targeted spraying of small mosquito-breeding areas rather than on blanketing an entire region with toxic pesticides. This would be safer for people and animals and would also cut down on mosquito resistance. Mosquito control experts determined that the best way of accomplishing this is to start eradication programs in the winter, when mosquitoes hibernate, rather than waiting until the creatures become active in warmer weather.

Efforts to locate and destroy overwintering mosquitoes in buildings, tunnels, and other common hibernation sites began. Durland Fish emphasized the importance of these measures in 2000, when he told the U.S. Congress, "Every conceivable effort must be made to control virus transmission early enough to prevent human infection and avoid the use of widespread aerial insecticide application to control an epidemic in humans. A repeat of last season's response must be avoided at all costs."[40]

Insecticide Concerns

The reason experts such as Fish believe that widespread aerial spraying should be avoided is that even though insecticides used in the United States must comply with regulations set by the U.S. Environmental Protection Agency (EPA), these chemicals are still poisons, and many doctors are concerned that children, elderly people, and people with chemical sensitivities in particular are likely to become ill with asthma or with immune or neurological disorders when exposed. Pesticides are also known to cause birth defects and are dangerous for animals.

Although localities throughout the United States now attempt to control mosquito populations using methods other than insecticide spraying, these efforts are not always successful, and spraying is often performed in warm weather to prevent WNV outbreaks. Some physicians have expressed concerns that the increased use of pesticides since WNV came along is riskier than the virus itself. For example, a Chicago neurologist stated in a *Smithsonian* magazine article:

> The issue of risk-benefit is not very clear. Some people will get West Nile fever, and fewer will get meningitis or encephalitis, and fewer still will have permanent disability. Only a minority of a minority will have any residual effects. So if you play that algorithm out, the numbers get really small. Is wholesale spraying justified with a disease of this benignity [low risk]? You have dogs licking the grass and young children crawling through it. God knows what that will do to the [health] of our community.[41]

A helicopter sprays insecticide in Los Angeles. Although the chemicals help control mosquito-borne disease outbreaks, health officials worry that the chemicals will trigger other diseases in children, the elderly, and people with chemical sensitivities.

The CDC and other federal agencies, however, have assured the public that some use of insecticides is essential and that any risk from them is minimal. The CDC states, "Pesticides that can be used for mosquito control have been judged by the EPA not to pose an unreasonable risk to human health. People who are concerned about exposure to a pesticide, such as those with chemical sensitivity or breathing conditions such as asthma can reduce their potential for exposure by staying indoors during the application period (typically nighttime)."[42]

Personal Prevention Measures

In addition to the public measures used to prevent and control the spread of WNV, health officials stress that personal prevention measures, such as using insect repellents and repairing screens to prevent mosquito bites, are equally important. The CDC emphasizes that these types of individual measures to prevent mosquito bites are a critical part of the national strategy to control the spread of WNV. "The easiest and best way to avoid WNV is to prevent mosquito bites,"[43] states the CDC.

Insect repellents do not kill insects; they just prevent or discourage them from biting. The CDC recommends using any of a variety of spray-on or lotion, liquid repellents on skin, including those containing DEET (N,N-diethyl-meta-toluamide), picaridin, oil of lemon eucalyptus, or IR3535. Of all these repellents, DEET has been proved to be most effective in most situations. Factors that can influence the effectiveness of repellents include outdoor temperature, the amount a person perspires, and the concentration of the product. Stronger concentrations of active ingredients tend to make a product most effective and give the longest-lasting protection but also can be potentially toxic, particularly to children, so safety must be weighed when selecting a product.

DEET works by blocking smell receptors on mosquito antennae. Mosquitoes usually locate their target people and animals from odors on the skin and from the smell of carbon dioxide being exhaled through the mouth, and blocking their smell receptors prevents them from finding and biting living creatures. Other insect repellents work in a similar manner.

Insect Repellent Safety

Public health agencies state that using approved insect repellents to prevent mosquito bites is safe as long as package directions are followed. Some general rules to ensure safety include:

- Use only on exposed skin, not on skin under clothing.
- Do not use repellents on cuts or sores.
- Keep repellents away from the eyes and mouth, and carefully rub them around the ears.
- Never spray repellents on the face. Spray them on the hands and then carefully apply to the face.
- Never let small children touch repellents. An adult should apply the substance for a child.
- Only use repellents when outdoors. Wash them off with soap and water when returning indoors.
- Immediately wash off any repellent that causes a rash or itching. Do not use it again.
- Do not use products containing DEET on infants.
- Do not use products containing oil of lemon eucalyptus on children under age three.
- Use permethrin only on clothing or camping gear, not on skin. Wash clothing containing permethrin before wearing it again.

Proper use of approved insect repellents can reduce the incidence of West Nile virus.

Some cover up the smell of human skin with the scent of the repellent so mosquitoes are not attracted to the skin.

In addition to recommending the use of effective mosquito repellents on the skin, the CDC also advises people to use a repellent called permethrin on clothing, shoes, bed nets, and camping gear to help keep mosquitoes away. However, they emphasize that permethrin should never be applied to skin.

Many people have expressed concerns about the safety of insect repellents, including permethrin and repellents used on the skin, since the chemicals they contain are toxic and since keeping them away from eyes and mouths is essential. The CDC, however, states that these chemicals are safe when used according to package directions.

Many products besides those that are applied to the skin are rumored to repel mosquitoes, but the CDC says that most are not effective. Among those they specify as being ineffective are garlic or vitamin B_1 taken by mouth, ultrasonic devices that emit sound waves, backyard bug zappers, and wristbands containing repellents.

In educating the public about the importance of preventing mosquito bites, health experts point out that many people are tempted to skip using repellents if they are not going to be outdoors for a long time. However, doctors at the North Colorado Medical Center advise, "Mosquitoes don't care if you are outside for two minutes or two hours. Find a repellent that meets your needs and wear it every time you are outside!"[44]

Other Preventive Measures

In addition to advising people to use repellent protection against mosquitoes, public health agencies recommend other things individuals can do to prevent mosquito bites. These include avoiding places where mosquitoes gather, such as ponds and lakes, and staying indoors at dusk and dawn when these insects are most active. However, some species, such as *Aedes vexans*, are very active during the day, so measures other than staying indoors at dusk and dawn are needed to avoid being bitten. Mosquitoes can be attracted to perfumes and lotions, so not wearing fragrances when outdoors can help keep them

Avoiding areas with stagnant water and staying inside when mosquitoes are most active can help prevent infection with the West Nile virus.

away. Wearing long pants, long sleeves, and shoes and socks, even in hot weather, are other protective measures.

Around the house and yard, public health agencies encourage individuals to make sure that window and door screens do not have holes that mosquitoes can get through. Experts say that replacing regular outdoor lights with yellow lights can also keep mosquitoes away, since insects are not attracted to yellow light. Draining standing water, including that in basements, flower pots, buckets, and swimming pool covers to take away mosquito breeding areas is also advised. In discussing the need to remain vigilant about such measures, Anthony Fauci of the NIAID told a U.S. Senate subcommittee, "I go out in my own backyard; I live in Washington, D.C., and every few days, you see something there that has collected water, be it a flower pot or an innertube or whatever that the children play with, and you just make sure every day you go out and turn it over and do not leave any standing water, because that really makes an impact."[45]

Vaccines are one additional method of preventing WNV infection. Vaccines are drugs that prevent illness by introducing some inactivated virus proteins into the body to trigger the immune system to make antibodies. If the individual is later exposed to the virus, the antibodies prevent him or her from getting sick. Although scientists are testing vaccines for use in humans, none are yet approved for nonexperimental use. At this time there are, however, three WNV vaccines approved for use in horses. These are West Nile–Innovator, Vetera WNV vaccine, and Recombitek Equine West Nile virus vaccine. The first two vaccines are made by inactivating WNV with a chemical called formalin so it cannot cause disease when injected into a horse. The third vaccine combines WNV proteins with inactivated canary pox virus to create a drug that stimulates horses' immune systems to produce antibodies without making the animals sick. Veterinarians now recommend that all horses receive one of these vaccines for protection.

Testing and using safe, effective vaccines to prevent WNV infection in people is just one of the goals public health experts have named as priorities for the future. Devising other methods of controlling the spread of the virus and diminishing its impact on infected people and animals are also important goals for WNV researchers.

CHAPTER FIVE

The Future

Because of the continuing spread of WNV, it "is now the most common cause of epidemic viral encephalitis in the US, and it will likely remain an important cause of neurological disease for the forseeable future,"[46] states an article published by the American Society for Microbiology. To address this and other issues presented by WNV, public health agencies, universities, and drug manufacturers are conducting research that they hope will diminish the future impact of the virus on people and animals.

The NIAID is sponsoring much of the current research on WNV in the United States. According to the agency, a variety of studies is being conducted to better understand, prevent, control, and treat WNV infections. States the NIAID:

> Complex interactions between the virus, birds and other animals, and the environment have influenced the pattern of West Nile virus (WNV) emergence and distribution across the United States. The specific factors contributing to the emergence of WNV, however, are poorly understood. Knowledge of these principles is essential in planning strategies to prevent, treat, and control this disease. The goal of NIAID basic research on WNV is to develop a knowledge base to enable researchers to develop medical countermeasures against WNV.[47]

Basic research is research that may not have immediate applications to treatment or cures for a disease but that provides essential background information that can lead to breakthroughs in applied research. An example of one area of NIAID-sponsored basic research under way at several research centers is studies centered on investigating how WNV acts on the nervous system. In these studies, doctors are performing laboratory tests on WNV patients' blood, urine, and cerebrospinal fluid

A research team traps mosquitoes and catches birds to test for West Nile virus. Scientists are conducting a variety of studies to better understand, prevent, control, and treat West Nile infections.

and also doing imaging and neurological tests to assess the immediate and long-term biochemical effects of the virus. They are following patients' progress for a year or more after infection to gauge how patterns of virus activity correlate with patient symptoms and complications and are performing MRI scans to see how WNV changes the brain at certain stages of illness and recovery. The physicians are also measuring each individual's immune response to the virus and determining how this affects the severity of illness. Scientists hope that insight into how the virus affects cells and brain structures in different people will eventually lead to new treatments.

Another example of basic research is being performed by Alexander Khromykh and his colleagues at the University of Queensland in Australia. They are studying how flaviviruses such as WNV replicate. As Khromykh's university website states, "We are aiming at a better understanding of how these viruses replicate in the host and cause disease, which will help in the development of antiviral drugs."[48] Khromykh and his associates recently discovered that the Kunjin strain of WNV needs a type of messenger RNA called GATA4 mRNA in mosquitoes' cells in order to replicate. When the virus infects a mosquito, this triggers the mosquito's body to produce GATA4 mRNA, and then a small RNA section in the virus, called a micro-RNA, targets and uses GATA4 to begin its replication process. The researchers chose the name KUN-miR-1 for this particular micro-RNA. Further research revealed that removing KUN-miR-1 from the virus or removing GATA4 from mosquitoes reduces the ability of the virus to reproduce, and the investigators are conducting more studies to determine exactly how KUN-miR-1 influences GATA4 and how GATA4 allows the virus to begin replicating. They hope to use knowledge about these processes to develop drugs that stop the virus by interfering with biochemical steps that allow it to replicate.

Research into Treatment

In addition to the many basic research projects under way, scientists are also engaged in applied research that may have immediate applications for WNV illness prevention and treatment.

In the pursuit of an effective WNV treatment, several experimental drugs are currently under investigation in various phases of clinical trials.

Initially, scientists test new drugs on laboratory animals for safety and effectiveness. If a drug is found to be safe and effective in animals, a drug manufacturer can apply to the FDA for approval to begin clinical trials that test the drug on human volunteers. Three clinical trial phases that evaluate safety and effectiveness on increasingly larger groups of people must be satisfactorily completed before the FDA approves a medication for marketing and nonexperimental use. Clinical trials also involve administering a placebo, or fake drug that looks like the real thing, to a control group of people while the experimental group receives the actual medication. This allows doctors to assess whether perceived positive effects can be attributed to the drug itself rather than to the expectation that it will help.

To ensure that a drug is safe for use, clinical trials take many years to complete, and patients who are desperately ill and need immediate treatment may not be able to receive new drugs fast enough to help them unless they enroll in a clinical trial. In some cases, though, doctors will try using a drug such as interferon, which is already approved for other purposes, in a WNV patient before the drug is actually approved to treat WNV if they believe it may help. This is known as off-label use.

Drugs Being Tested

One new drug being tested for the prevention and treatment of brain or spinal cord inflammation in WNV patients is Omr-IgG, which is given intravenously. The Israeli company Omrix made Omr-IgG from antibodies found in the blood of people who have been infected with WNV. The drug is known as an immunoglobulin because it bolsters the immune system by adding specific synthetic antibodies to those that the body produces. Preliminary test results showed Omr-IgG to be safe, and current studies are evaluating its effectiveness in reducing brain inflammation in seriously ill patients and in preventing severe inflammation in infected people who are at high risk of

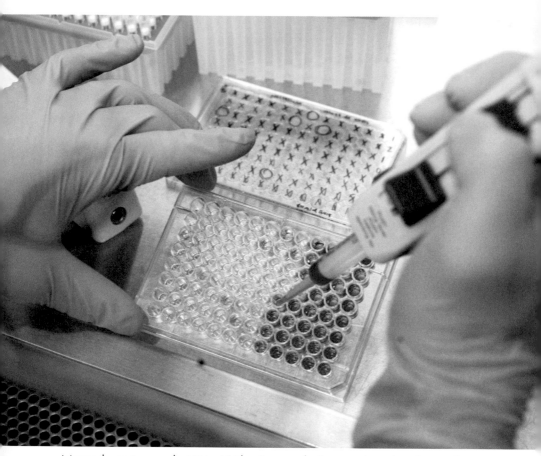

Many drugs to combat West Nile virus are being produced and tested. This researcher works for AVI BioPharma, which has developed a drug called Neugene that specifically targets West Nile virus.

developing serious complications. According to the NIAID, "Study investigators believe people who are not able to fight infection well may be at risk for developing neurologic problems (having to do with the brain, spinal cord, nerves, and muscles) if they get WNV infection."[49] Thus, the researchers are giving Omr-IgG to infected people who have immune diseases in hopes of boosting their immune systems so they can fight off the virus and avoid complications or death. The effectiveness of the drug is being assessed with brain scans, neurological function tests, and blood tests.

Another new intravenous drug being tested for treatment of neuroinvasive WNV is AVI-4020. Previous studies showed that AVI-4020 crosses the blood-brain barrier, and a current study is assessing how fast this happens and how much of the drug gets into the central nervous system. Finding drugs that can cross the blood-brain barrier is challenging, and if AVI-4020 proves to do this quickly and effectively, it could potentially eradicate the virus before the virus does significant damage to the brain. This would represent tremendous progress in the fight against neuroinvasive WNV. AVI-4020 works by interfering with WNV translation, which means that it binds to the virus RNA to prevent the genetic instructions from being expressed. As a result, the virus cannot reproduce. Drugs like AVI-4020 that interfere with RNA are known as antisense compounds because they prevent viruses or other targeted cells from making sense of genetic instructions.

Another new drug, MGAWN1, works against WNV in an entirely different way. MGAWN1 is a monoclonal antibody—a genetically engineered antibody made by cloning a natural antibody to the virus. The antibody recognizes a protein called the E protein on the WNV envelope and latches onto this protein. This signals the body's immune system to destroy the virus.

Researchers at Washington University in St. Louis originally developed the anti-WNV antibody that later became MGAWN1 in 2005 and tested it on mice, with excellent results. "We could give this antibody to mice as long as five days after infection, when West Nile virus had entered the brain, and it could still cure them. It also completely protected them against death,"[50] stated one of the researchers in *NIH News*. Scientists affiliated with the biotechnology firm Macrogenics later created the monoclonal antibody MGAWN1 from this antibody and are now testing it on humans.

An early clinical trial in healthy adults showed that MGAWN1 was tolerated fairly well by people, though it did affect blood sugar levels and blood cell counts, and it sometimes caused headaches and sinus problems. The drug inactivated WNV in most of the people in this study. Further studies will evaluate ideal doses and further assess safety and effectiveness. In discussing scientists' hopes for MGAWN1's effectiveness in severely ill patients, researcher Russell Bartt of Rush University Medical Center said in a news release, "This new drug therapy has the potential of neutralizing the virus and could possibly reduce or prevent complications associated with the West Nile virus neuroinvasive disease. This could represent a significant advancement for patients with West Nile."[51]

Vaccine Research

A great deal of research is directed at formulating and testing WNV vaccines as well as at developing effective treatment drugs. The vaccines under current investigation for use in humans are either chimeric vaccines, DNA vaccines, or vaccines containing cocktails of individual WNV proteins. Most of these experimental vaccines target the virus envelope's E glycoprotein, which is the major surface protein that triggers antibody production by the human immune system.

Chimeric vaccines combine genes from more than one virus into a single vaccine. That way the vaccine can be used to prevent diseases caused by similar viruses. A chimeric vaccine known as ChimeriVax-WN02 contains genes from WNV and yellow fever virus. To create it scientists took an already-approved yellow fever vaccine and replaced some of the yellow fever virus genes with genes that code for two WNV surface proteins. Phase 2 (which tests the drug on fewer than 100 people) clinical trials reported in 2011 showed the vaccine to be safe and effective in preventing infection in healthy adults aged eighteen to forty. Results in adults older than forty found it to be effective as well, but more likely to cause adverse side effects such as fatigue, headache, and muscle pain in people in this age group. Larger clinical trials are under way.

Another chimeric vaccine under investigation, WN/DEN-43'delta30, uses a weakened dengue virus that carries WNV genes in order to induce an immune response. Alexander Pletnev and his colleagues at the NIAID developed WN/DEN43'delta30 by replacing outer-shell proteins in the dengue virus with proteins from WNV. They then weakened the combination by deleting some of the dengue virus RNA so it would not be able to replicate. Dengue

Alexander Pletnev

Microbiologist Alexander Pletnev of the NIAID and his colleagues developed a new technique for mixing parts of two viruses together to form chimeric vaccines in 1991. Pletnev's team discovered that creating a chimeric vaccine could render an infectious virus incapable of causing disease but at the same time would also trigger a strong immune response when injected into a human or animal. This work led to Pletnev's later development of the first chimeric WNV vaccine using WNV and dengue virus in 2002. In announcing the successful use of the new vaccine, WN/DEN43'delta30, to prevent WNV in monkeys in 2003, NIAID director Anthony Fauci stated in *NIH News*, "Because our researchers have more than a decade of experience working with this class of virus, they could respond very quickly to the urgent public health need for a promising West Nile virus vaccine." This vaccine is now being tested in human clinical trials.

Born in Russia, Pletnev obtained a PhD in chemistry in 1983 and doctorate of science degrees in biochemistry and molecular biology in 1990 from the Russian Academy of Sciences. He joined the Laboratory of Infectious Diseases at the NIAID in 1991 and is now chief of the Neurotropic Flavivirus Section, where he continues his work on developing new vaccines.

Quoted in National Institute of Allergy and Infectious Diseases. "Promising West Nile Virus Vaccine Protects Monkeys." *NIH News*, August 18, 2003. www.niaid.nih .gov/news/newsreleases/2003/Pages/wnv.aspx.

virus was chosen for this vaccine partly because it is a flavivirus that does not infect the brain, so combining dengue with WNV meant the resulting vaccine would be unlikely to affect people's nervous system.

Tests on mice and monkeys showed that injecting WN/DEN-43'delta30 stimulated the production of WNV antibodies, and when the animals were later exposed to WNV, they did not get sick. Doctors at the Johns Hopkins University School of Public Health are now conducting Phase 2 clinical trials in humans

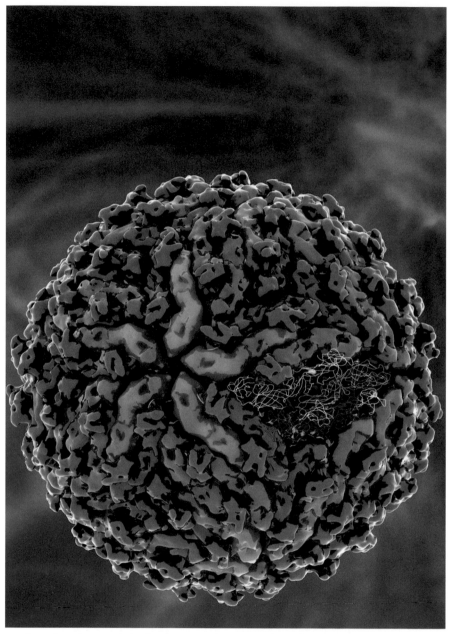

A molecular model of a dengue virus particle is shown. Because the dengue virus does not infect the brain, parts of the dengue virus are being combined with parts of the West Nile virus to create a West Nile vaccine that will not negatively affect the patient's nervous system.

to assess the safety and effectiveness of different dosages of the vaccine.

In contrast to chimeric vaccines, which use inactivated viruses, DNA vaccines introduce only DNA into the recipient. No DNA vaccines are currently approved for use in people, but several are available for veterinary use, including a West Nile DNA vaccine for horses. Scientists make DNA vaccines by removing a strand of RNA from a virus to kill the virus. Then the RNA strand is converted to a DNA strand that encodes instructions for making a WNV antigen. When this DNA is injected into a person or animal, the body reads the DNA instructions and produces WNV antigens, which then trigger the immune system to produce antibodies to the antigens. DNA vaccines are unique in that they induce the recipient to produce both antigens and antibodies.

Two similar DNA vaccines, called VRC-WNVDNA017-00-VP and VRC-WNVDNA020-00-VP, are being tested by the NIAID in clinical trials. The NIAID writes about WNVDNA020-00-VP, "The vaccine used in this study contains DNA that instructs the body to produce a small amount of a protein found in WNV. If the body creates resistance or immunity to these proteins, then the vaccine may protect against WNV."[52] Phase 1 clinical trials on a handful of volunteers indicated that both vaccines seem safe, and blood tests on participants revealed that both promoted the production of antibodies to WNV in most people. Current studies are being conducted on more subjects, and the researchers are also using blood tests to assess whether genetic differences in people who receive the vaccines affect how the immune system responds.

In addition to the vaccines being tested in clinical trials, there are several compounds being developed that are not yet far enough along for testing on humans. For example, scientists at the University of Texas have started testing a live, weakened WNV vaccine called RepliVaxWN on mice and hamsters, and preliminary results show that a single dose protects the animals from becoming infected with WNV for at least six months. RepliVaxWN is made of pieces of WNV that scientists manipulate so the virus can only replicate one time. In other research on live, weakened virus vaccines, investigators at the University of Queensland in Australia have developed a vaccine based on the Kunjin strain of WNV that they are now testing on laboratory animals. Results with mice indicate that the animals produce antibodies to both Kunjin and WNV after receiving the Kunjin vaccine. The researchers write, "West Nile and Kunjin have similar genetic sequences, but Kunjin produces only rare, non-fatal cases of disease and as such provides an extremely stable vaccine."[53]

Research on Birds

In addition to studying human vaccines against WNV, scientists are also looking into whether vaccinating birds will help control the spread of the disease. In 2008 researchers at the University of California–Santa Cruz and at the Smithsonian Migratory Bird Center launched a study to determine whether vaccinating robins, which have played a major role in spreading WNV to mosquitoes in the United States, would slow the spread of the virus. Biologists caught wild robins in nets and vaccinated them with an approved horse WNV vaccine. They also vaccinated baby birds in nests. Following the vaccinations, the scientists found that the vaccinated birds were not infectious, meaning that they did not transmit WNV to mosquitoes that bit them even if the birds were infected with the virus. The robins also developed antibodies to WNV, so they did not become ill when later exposed to the virus.

Vaccinating these robins reduced the number of infected mosquitoes in the study area by about 64 percent. According to an article in the Smithsonian Migratory Bird Center newsletter, "This was a substantial reduction in the transmission of the disease and a promising solution for the future. However, capturing and hand-vaccinating birds is time-consuming and labor-intensive. In the future, the team would like to develop a more feasible solution for large-scale vaccination, such as the development of a vaccine the birds find appetizing to eat."[54]

Other studies are assessing the effectiveness of vaccinating other types of birds such as crows and hawks. A study reported in 2011 in the *Journal of the American Veterinary Association,*

Researchers inspect a robin, one species decimated by West Nile virus. Scientists are researching whether vaccinating birds would help reduce the spread of West Nile virus.

for example, found that vaccinating red-tailed hawks with a DNA vaccine was safe but did not prevent the birds from getting sick if they became infected. Further tests are planned.

Researchers are also attempting to learn more about exactly how certain birds are spreading WNV. Scientists hope new research will lead to information that can help wildlife biologists target vaccines or other preventive measures appropriately. Toward this end, the National Wildlife Health Center associated with the U.S. Geological Survey is conducting research on a variety of wild birds. Studies on greater sage-grouse in the western United States, for instance, are evaluating whether these birds are spreading WNV and whether declining populations of the bird are related to WNV infection. Scientists are testing blood samples from these birds and from birds that live near them to find out whether they are infected with WNV. Thus far, these studies have not led to any conclusions about greater sage-grouse but have led biologists to conclude that vesper sparrows and chukar partridge, which commonly live near greater sage-grouse, are resistant to becoming very sick from WNV infection.

This information has led the researchers to believe that vesper sparrows and chukar partridge that survive a WNV infection may be contributing to the spread of WNV to mosquitoes in Wyoming, Montana, Oregon, and other western states. Blood tests on these birds have shown high viremia levels that could easily be transmitting the virus when the birds are bitten by mosquitoes, and further studies are under way to try to determine whether this is indeed happening. The scientists are also interested in studying factors that seem to prevent the birds from getting severely sick or dying from high viremia.

U.S. Geological Survey scientists have also learned that the intensity and speed of WNV transmission may be affected by stress in wild birds. As researchers at the National Wildlife Health Center explain:

> During the course of daily life, wild birds are periodically exposed to environmental stressors such as breeding activities, migration, food-shortages and predation [attacks by predators]. When a wild bird is reacting to one or more of these conditions, its ability to fight viral infection such as WNV may be reduced. We are investigating the effects of certain stressors to better define the relationship between stress and a bird's response to WNV because stressed birds may be immune suppressed, carry more virus, and thus more likely infect mosquito vectors.[55]

The investigators are measuring stress levels in certain birds and trying to determine whether high stress levels increase their susceptibility to WNV infection. They believe this knowledge may help biologists identify which birds are most likely to spread WNV to mosquitoes that bite humans.

This golden eagle was just vaccinated against West Nile virus. Scientists have learned that the intensity and speed of West Nile transmission may be affected by how much stress wild birds experience.

Other Factors Affecting Disease Transmission

Other studies on WNV transmission are also investigating how birds, mosquitoes, and the environment interact to increase the spread of the virus. For example, researchers at Oregon State University and the University of Florida are conducting studies that have revealed that certain weather patterns have increased the intensity of virus transmission in south Florida. The researchers plan to pursue similar studies in other areas of the United States. Through their studies, the researchers found that simply looking at total rainfall is not an accurate method of predicting mosquito activity and virus transmission in a given year. Instead, patterns of rainfall interacting with certain types of birds and mosquitoes in a particular area are critical in this process. As researcher Jeffrey Shaman explains in an Oregon State University publication:

> In some cases, rain can actually help control mosquitoes by flushing away larval habitats. And simply having more mosquitoes doesn't necessarily mean that we'll experience a greater incidence of West Nile Virus. The mosquitoes themselves must first be infected with the virus. Researchers call the process through which more mosquitoes become infected "amplification," and there are a number of factors that lead to that stage. By identifying these factors in the wild, it will enhance our ability to create control strategies.[56]

Shaman and his colleagues discovered that, at least in southern Florida, a dry spring followed by a very wet summer is one factor that vastly increases this amplification process. This occurs because a drought early in the year leads mosquitoes that survive to breed in dense, moist, forested areas, where many birds that happen to transmit WNV nest in the springtime. The resident mosquitoes then feed on the nesting birds over and over in these small areas, and each bird can thus infect many mosquitoes. The scientists call this phenomenon "drought-induced amplification." When the spring drought is followed by a rainy summer, the infected mosquitoes that were confined to the moist forest areas move to other nearby places and go on to infect many animals and people. The fact that the mosquito species in Florida that prefer feeding on birds are the same ones that favor biting humans has also contributed to the rapid spread of WNV in this area under these conditions.

Shaman points out that the different characteristics of other regions can lead to completely different amplification patterns. He states, "In almost all cases, the amplification of West Nile Virus will start with mosquitoes that carry the disease mingling

Prevention and Control Requires More than Vaccines

While much WNV research is devoted to finding safe, effective vaccines, researcher Duane J. Gubler emphasizes in a 2011 article in the journal Expert Review of Vaccines *that vaccination is not the only measure needed to successfully control WNV in the future:*

Our success in preventing and controlling flavivirus diseases in the past 30 years has been disappointing. There are many reasons for this poor performance including lack of political will, lack of research and misguided public health policies, combined with the global trends of unprecedented human population growth, unplanned urbanization, and globalization.... Many public health officials see vaccination as the answer. Vaccines will definitely help, but are not the panacea [cure-all]. Used alone, they too will probably fail to control the disease because of cost and lack of coverage in the large tropical cities of resource-poor countries. . . . Sustainable prevention and control of this disease in the future will probably require an integrated approach that uses vaccines, mosquito control, environmental management, antivirals and good clinical diagnosis and management.

Duane J. Gubler. "Emerging Vector-Borne Flavivirus Diseases: Are Vaccines the Solution?" *Expert Review of Vaccines*, May 2011, pp. 563–565.

An inspector in Florida collects mosquito larvae from a standing pool of water. Florida researchers have found that a dry spring followed by a very wet summer increases the number of West Nile-infected mosquitoes.

with birds that are good carriers. How fast and far it spreads from there depends on weather, terrain, vegetation, humidity, the types of birds that live in the region and even the number of housing developments in a given area. These are the variables that need to be studied across the country."[57]

The Future and West Nile Virus

As studies continue on the birds, mosquitoes, and other factors affecting the spread of WNV, as well as on prevention and treatment, health experts say the future impact and transmission of the virus is unknown. Data gathered in 2008 and reported by the CDC in 2010 gave some epidemiologists hope that the intensity of virus spread and the incidence of severe WNV disease may be waning, but most believe it is impossible to predict whether or not these trends will continue. This data indicated that cases of neuroinvasive WNV infections decreased from 1.02 cases per 100,000 in 2002 to 0.23 cases per 100,000 in 2008 in the United States. The researchers who conducted the study wrote, "Whether the incidence reported in 2008 represents a decrease that will continue is unknown; variations in vectors, amplifying hosts, human activity, and environmental factors make predicting future WNV transmission levels difficult."[58]

Despite the fact that no one knows what direction the WNV epidemic will take, public health officials point out that the knowledge gained from studying and developing strategies to control this invasion in the United States can be used not only to contain WNV, but also to better respond to future threats from other emerging viruses. An article by California State University–East Bay biology professor Helen M. Sowers states, "Yet again the international spread of a disease that was formerly restricted to a small area shows how vulnerable the entire world is to emerging diseases. We must be constantly prepared to investigate such new-to-us maladies. West Nile virus is an example of our shrinking globe and how a tipping point—a critical mass or condition—can start an epidemic."[59]

Notes

Introduction: A Spreading Invasion

1. U.S. General Accounting Office/Health, Education, and Human Services Division. *West Nile Virus Outbreak: Lessons for Public Health Preparedness*. Washington, DC: US General Accounting Office, 2000, p. 8.
2. Stephen S. Hall. "On the Trail of the West Nile Virus." *Smithsonian*, July 2003. www.smithsonianmag.com/science-nature /westnile.html?c=y&page=1.
3. Quoted in Hall. "On the Trail of the West Nile Virus."

Chapter One: What Is West Nile Virus?

4. James Pile. "West Nile Fever: Here to Stay and Spreading." *Cleveland Clinic Journal of Medicine*, June 2001, p. 554.
5. Doug E. Brackney, Jennifer E. Beane, and Gregory D. Ebel. "RNAi Targeting of West Nile Virus in Mosquito Midguts Promotes Virus Diversification." *PLoS Pathogens*, July 3, 2009. www.plospathogens.org/article/info%3Adoi%2F10 .1371%2Fjournal.ppat.1000502.
6. Marina De Filette, Sebastian Ulbert, Mike Diamond, and Nick N. Sanders. "Recent Progress in West Nile Virus Diagnosis and Vaccination." *Veterinary Research*, January 2012. http://digitalcommons.wustl.edu/open_access_pubs/854.
7. U.S. General Accounting Office/Health, Education, and Human Services Division. *West Nile Virus Outbreak*, p. 14.
8. National Institutes of Health. "Promising New West Nile Therapy Cures Disease in Mice." *NIH News*, April 24, 2005. www.niaid.nih.gov/news/newsreleases/2005/Pages/westnile therapy.aspx.
9. Quoted in U.S. Senate Committee on Governmental Affairs. *Responding to the Public Health Threat of West Nile Virus*. Memphis, TN: Books, 2011, p. 18.

10. Centers for Disease Control and Prevention. "West Nile Virus: Epidemiological Information for Clinicians." www .cdc.gov/ncidod/dvbid/westnile/clinicians/epi.htm.

11. Shannan L. Rossi, Ted M. Ross, and Jared D. Evans. "West Nile Virus." *Clinical Laboratory Medicine*, March 2010, p. 54.

12. Centers for Disease Control and Prevention. "West Nile Virus: Clinical Description." www.cdc.gov/ncidod/dvbid/west nile/clinicians/clindesc.htm#fever.

Chapter Two: How West Nile Virus Is Spread

13. Tony L. Goldberg, Travis K. Anderson, and Gabriel L. Hamer. "West Nile Virus May Have Hitched a Ride Across the Western United States on *Culex tarsalis* Mosquitoes." *Molecular Ecology*, March 29, 2010, p. 1518.

14. Quoted in ScienceDaily. "West Nile Virus Transmission Linked to Land Use Patterns and 'Super-Spreaders,'" October 20, 2011. www.sciencedaily.com/releases/2011/10/111 020145050.htm.

15. Rossi et al. "West Nile Virus," p. 49.

16. Quoted in ScienceDaily. "West Nile Virus Transmission Linked to Land Use Patterns and 'Super-Spreaders.'"

17. Quoted in U.S. Senate Subcommittee on Environment and Public Works. *West Nile Virus*. Washington, DC: US Government Printing Office, 2000, p. 57.

18. Hall. "On the Trail of the West Nile Virus." *Smithsonian*, July 2003. www.smithsonianmag.com/science-nature/westnile .html?c=y&page=9

19. Quoted in U.S. Senate Subcommittee on Environment and Public Works. *West Nile Virus*, p. 20.

20. Michael S. Diamond. "Virus and Host Determinants of West Nile Virus Pathogenesis." *PLoS Pathogens*, June 26, 2009. www.plospathogens.org/article/info%3Adoi%2F10.1371%2F journal.ppat.1000452.

21. Quoted in U.S. Senate Subcommittee on Environment and Public Works. *West Nile Virus*, p. 21.

22. Quoted in U.S. Senate Committee on Governmental Affairs. *Responding to the Public Health Threat of West Nile Virus,* p. 34.

Chapter Three: Treatment for and Living with West Nile Virus

23. Centers for Disease Control and Prevention. "West Nile Virus: What You Need to Know." www.cdc.gov/ncidod /dvbid/westnile/WNV_factsheet.htm.
24. Melanie A. Samuel and Michael S. Diamond. "Alpha/Beta Interferon Protects Against Lethal West Nile Virus Infection by Restricting Cellular Tropism and Enhancing Neuronal Survival." *Journal of Virology,* November 2005. www.ncbi.nlm.nih.gov/pmc/articles/PMC1262587.
25. Quoted in West Nile Virus Survivors Foundation. "West Nile Virus Survivor Stories from the West Nile Virus Survivors Foundation: Chris Cottrell WI." http://westnilesurvivorstories .blogspot.com.
26. Quoted in Encephalitis Global Support Community. "16 Yr. Old Recovering from West Nile Enceph," May 15, 2011. www.inspire.com/groups/encephalitis-global/discussion /16yr-old-recovering-from-west-nile-enceph.
27. Quoted in West Nile Virus Survivors Foundation. "West Nile Virus Survivor Stories from the West Nile Virus Survivors Foundation: Ken Speake; In His Own Words—MN(2)." http://westnilesurvivorstories.blogspot.com.
28. ScienceDaily. "Severe West Nile Infection Could Lead to Lifetime of Symptoms," March 17, 2008. www.sciencedaily .com/releases/2008/03/080317134259.htm.
29. Quoted in ScienceDaily. "Severe West Nile Infection Could Lead to Lifetime of Symptoms."
30. Quoted in West Nile Virus Survivors Foundation. "West Nile Virus Survivor Stories from the West Nile Virus Survivors Foundation: Richard Gibson, CA Survivor." http://westnilc survivorstories.blogspot.com.
31. Quoted in Barineau Heating and Air Conditioning. "Fund Established to Support Family of West Nile Victim." www .barineauac.com/daniel-williams-fund.

32. Quoted in West Nile Virus Survivors Foundation. "West Nile Virus Survivor Stories from the West Nile Virus Survivors Foundation: David Kelly, SC Survivor." http://westnilesurvivor stories.blogspot.com/2007_11_01_archive.html.

33. Quoted in West Nile Virus Survivors Foundation. "West Nile Virus Survivor Stories from the West Nile Virus Survivors Foundation: Mel Lacy, ID." http://westnilesurvivorstories .blogspot.com.

34. Richard Lyon. "My West Nile Story." Yahoo! Voices, April 9, 2008. http://voices.yahoo.com/my-west-nile-story-1350609 .html.

Chapter Four: Prevention and Control

35. Quoted in U.S. Senate Subcommittee on Environment and Public Works. *West Nile Virus*, p. 5.

36. Quoted in U.S. Senate Subcommittee on Environment and Public Works. *West Nile Virus*, p. 6.

37. U.S. General Accounting Office/Health, Education, and Human Services Division. *West Nile Virus Outbreak*, p. 18.

38. Centers for Disease Control and Prevention. "Epidemic/ Epizootic West Nile Virus in the United States: Guidelines for Surveillance, Prevention, and Control." www.cdc.gov /ncidod/dvbid/westnile/resources/wnv-guidelines-aug-2003.pdf.

39. Quoted in U.S. Senate Subcommittee on Environment and Public Works. *West Nile Virus*, p. 10.

40. Quoted in U.S. Senate Subcommittee on Environment and Public Works. *West Nile Virus*, p. 32.

41. Quoted in Hall. "On the Trail of the West Nile Virus." *Smithsonian*, July 2003. www.smithsonianmag.com/science-nature /westnile.html?c=y&page=5

42. Centers for Disease Control and Prevention. "Pesticides Used in Mosquito Control." www.cdc.gov/ncidod/dvbid /westnile/qa/pesticides.htm.

43. Centers for Disease Control and Prevention. "West Nile Virus: What You Need to Know."

44. North Colorado Medical Center. "West Nile Virus (WNV)." www.bannerhealth.com/Locations/Colorado/North+Colorado

+Medical+Center/Programs+and+Services/Emergency+and
+Trauma+Care/_West+Nile+Virus.htm.
45. Quoted in U.S. Senate Committee on Governmental Affairs. *Responding to the Public Health Threat of West Nile Virus*, p. 12.

Chapter Five: The Future

46. John H. Beigel et al. "Safety and Pharmokinetics of Single Intravenous Dose of MGAWN1, a Novel Monoclonal Antibody to West Nile Virus." *Antimicrobial Agents Chemotherapy*, March 29, 2010. http://aac.asm.org/content/early/2010 /03/29/AAC.01178-09.full.pdf.
47. National Institute of Allergy and Infectious Diseases. "West Nile Virus." www.niaid.nih.gov/topics/westnile/research/pages/basic.aspx.
48. Alexander Khromykh. "Professor Alexander Khromykh." University of Queensland. www.scmb.uq.edu.au/staff/alexander -khromykh.
49. Clinical Trials.gov. "IVIG—West Nile Encephalitis: Safety and Efficacy." http://clinicaltrials.gov/show/NCT00068055.
50. Quoted in National Institutes of Health. "Promising New West Nile Therapy Cures Disease in Mice."
51. Quoted in Rush University Medical Center. "Study to Examine New Treatment for West Nile Virus." www.rush.edu /rumc/page-1277738458481.html.
52. Clinical Trials.gov. "Vaccine to Prevent West Nile Virus Disease." www.clinicaltrials.gov/ct/show/nct00106769?order=6.
53. University of Queensland. "West Nile Breakthrough." www .uq.edu.au/research/index.html?page=13269&pid=0.
54. Tina Gheen. "Slowing the Spread of West Nile Virus: The Robin Vaccination Study." Smithsonian National Zoological Park Migratory Bird Center. http://nationalzoo.si.edu/scbi /migratorybirds/science_article/default.cfm?id=48.
55. National Wildlife Health Center. "West Nile Virus Research." www.nwhc.usgs.gov/disease_information/west _nile_virus/research_projects.jsp.
56. Quoted in Oregon State University. "'Amplification' Strategy May Be Key to Combating West Nile Virus." http://ocean

andair.coas.oregonstate.edu/index.cfm?fuseaction=content .display&pageID=92.

57. Quoted in Oregon State University. "'Amplification' Strategy May Be Key to Combating West Nile Virus."

58. Nicole P. Lindsey et al. "Surveillance for Human West Nile Virus Disease—United States, 1999–2008." Centers for Disease Control and Prevention. www.cdc.gov/mmwr/preview/mmwrhtml/ss5902a1.htm.

59. Helen M. Sowers. "Update on West Nile Virus." California Association for Medical Laboratory Technicians. www.camlt.org/pdf_files/forms/976-form.pdf.

Glossary

antibody: A chemical produced by the immune system to fight a specific antigen.

antigen: A foreign substance or organism that triggers the immune system to produce antibodies when the antigen enters the body.

arbovirus: A virus that is spread by bloodsucking arthropods.

blood-brain barrier: A biological mechanism that prevents most harmful substances from reaching the brain.

cerebrospinal fluid: The liquid that surrounds the brain and spinal cord.

encephalitis: A brain inflammation.

endemic: Always present.

epidemic: A large outbreak of disease.

epidemiologist: A doctor who specializes in tracking and controlling epidemics of illness.

flavivirus: A family of arboviruses that includes West Nile virus.

meninges: The lining of the brain.

meningitis: An inflammation of the lining of the brain.

meningoencephalitis: An inflammation of the brain and meninges.

neuroinvasive: Tending to invade, such as a virus, the nervous system.

neurological: Pertaining to the nervous system.

neuron: A nerve cell.

pathogen: An organism that causes disease.

surveillance: Monitoring to assess whether a problem is worsening.

vaccine: A drug given to stimulate an immune response to prevent a disease.

vector: The agent that transmits something such as a virus.

ventilator: A machine that breathes for a person who cannot breathe by him- or herself.

viremia: The concentration of a virus in the blood of an infected person or animal.

virus: A submicroscopic organism that needs a living host to survive.

West Nile poliomyelitis: A type of neuroinvasive WNV that involves inflammation of the spinal cord.

West Nile virus (WNV): A flavivirus that can cause mild to severe disease.

Organizations to Contact

Centers for Disease Control and Prevention (CDC)
1600 Clifton Rd.
Atlanta, GA 30333
Phone: (800) 232-4636
Website: www.cdc.gov

The CDC is the primary federal public health agency involved with providing public health information, as well as with monitoring and controlling WNV.

National Institute of Allergy and Infectious Diseases (NIAID)
NIAID Office of Communications and Government Relations
6610 Rockledge Dr., MSC 6612
Bethesda, MD 20892-6612
Phone: (866) 284-4107
Website: www.niaid.nih.gov

The NIAID is the branch of the National Institutes of Health that conducts research into infectious diseases, including WNV. It also provides public information on all aspects of the disease.

U.S. Department of Agriculture (USDA)
Animal Welfare Information Center
National Agricultural Library
10301 Baltimore Ave., Rm. 410
Beltsville, MD 20705
Phone: (301) 504-6212
Website: www.awic.nal.usda.gov

The USDA's Animal and Plant Health Inspection Services and Animal Welfare Information Center provides information on how WNV affects animals.

U.S. Geological Survey (USGS)
U.S. Department of the Interior
1849 C St. NW
Washington, DC 20240
Phone: (888) 275-8747
Website: www.usgs.gov

The USGS monitors and conducts research on natural resources and life sciences in the United States. With respect to WNV, the USGS studies the environmental influences on disease spread and its effects on animals.

World Health Organization (WHO)
Avenue Appia 20
1211 Geneva 27
Switzerland
Phone: +41 22 791 21 11
Website: www.who.int

As the health authority for the United Nations, WHO provides information and leadership concerning global health matters. The organization provides extensive information about WNV.

For More Information

Books

John DiConsiglio. *Blood Suckers! Deadly Mosquito Bites*. New York: Scholastic, 2007. A book written for teens about many mosquito-borne illnesses.

Jeffrey Sfakianos and Alan Hecht. *West Nile Virus*. New York: Chelsea House, 2009. Written for teens, this book covers all aspects of WNV.

Emily Smucker. *Emily: My True Story of Chronic Illness and Missing Out on Life*. Deerfield Beach, FL: Health Communications, 2009. The true story of a teen's struggles with WNV.

Internet Sources

CBC News. "West Nile Virus: Facts and Figures," September 10, 2009. www.cbc.ca/news/health/story/2009/09/10/f-west-nile-virus-background-facts-figures.html.

Mayo Clinic. "West Nile Virus." www.mayoclinic.com/health/west-nile-virus/DS00438.

MedlinePlus. "West Nile Virus." www.nlm.nih.gov/medlineplus/ency/article/007186.htm.

Websites

Encephalitis, Teens Health from Nemours (http://kidshealth.org/teen/infections/bacterial_viral/encephalitis.html). A teen website about encephalitis, which can result from WNV infection.

West Nile Virus, Family Doctor.org (http://familydoctor.org/familydoctor/en/diseases-conditions/west-nile-virus.html). Overview of symptoms, causes, treatment, and prevention of WNV from family doctors.

West Nile Virus Overview, Discovery Fit & Health (http://health.howstuffworks.com/diseases-conditions/infectious/west-nile-virus1.htm). This site provides an easily understood overview of WNV.

West Nile Virus, Teens Health from Nemours (http://kids health.org/teen/infections/bacterial_viral/west_nile.html). A teen website from the nonprofit Nemours Foundation that explains all aspects of WNV.

Index

Picture Credits

About the Author

Melissa Abramovitz has been a writer since 1986 and has published hundreds of nonfiction magazine articles for all age groups, along with numerous short stories, poems, and educational books for children and teens. She also writes children's picture books and is the author of an acclaimed book for writers.